Forex Trading for Beginners

Proven Strategies to Succeed and Create Passive Income with Forex

Introduction to Forex Swing Trading, Day Trading, Options, Futures & ETFs

Table of contents

Introduction

In the past, the forex market was only reserved and exclusive to financial firms, big companies, billionaires, central banks, and hedge funds.

But through the emergence of digital banking and the rise of smartphones, anyone can now participate in this volatile, highly liquid, and exciting financial market.

Successful forex traders are now making big bucks every day, thanks to the availability of forex platforms.

But in my years of experience in the forex world, I also encountered people who have lost a lot of money within minutes.

Certainly, the forex market can make you rich, but not overnight. It still takes knowledge, skills, and discipline in following the most suitable strategies before you can become profitable in the forex market.

Written as a beginner's guide for people who are enticed to join the forex market, this book can help you learn the following:

- The fundamental theories and mechanisms behind the forex market

- The essential skills you need to learn to become successful in forex trading

- The top fundamental and technical strategies that seasoned forex traders are using

- The common mistakes that you must avoid so you will not lose money

The forex world can become a fertile ground for day traders. But this can only be possible if you really understand the basic concepts that influence the biggest financial market in the world.

The objective in writing this beginner's guide is to help you develop a good understanding of the forex market before you even start trading.

Let's get started.

Chapter 1. Brief History of the Forex Market

"Risk comes from not knowing what you're doing." -
Warren Buffett

With the worldwide scale of the forex market, you need first to understand important historical events, which are related to the currency system we use today, as well as how the forex market has evolved over time before you try trading or investing in this highly volatile market.

The Gold Standard

The Gold Standard model was established in 1875 as a global currency model. This became one of the early milestones of the forex market. Prior to this standard, countries in the 19th century usually used precious metals like gold or silver for international payments.

The main disadvantage of this system is the volatility of gold and silver prices as they are influenced by the supply and demand. For example, depletion of primary gold reserves in a specific country can have lasting effects on the prices of gold.

In the gold standard, governments or companies have to agree to convert their currencies into specific equivalent of gold and vice versa. Hence, the currency should be backed by actual gold in reserve. And so, the governments during the 19th century had to secure sufficient gold reserves to catch up with the demand for exchanging foreign currencies.

Leading world economies of that time such as Great Britain and China had already established the value of currency. Eventually, the distinction in the price of gold between two currencies was regarded as the rate of exchange between the two currencies. This became the early standard for trading currencies.

At the onset of World War I, the gold standard eventually became obsolete. Because of imminent danger from the Axis Power, many European countries had to finance massive military projects. Gold reserves were not enough as they needed to complete the project within a limited timeframe.

After the war, some countries re-established the gold standard, but most economies discarded the system when war again erupted in the 1940s. However, gold continued to be valued as the preferred channel for international payments.

The USD Standard

Before the end of World War II, the Allied Forces deemed it crucial to establish a currency system to solve the downsides of the gold standard. So in 1944, a meeting was convened at Bretton Woods, NH to deliberate on a new currency management system. The resulting system was later on called the Bretton Woods System.

The Allied Forces agree to adhere to the following:

- Use a fixed rate system for trading currencies

- Use the United States Dollar as the primary reserve currency to replace gold

- Form three worldwide agencies to manage economic activities: the International Monetary Fund (IMF), the World Bank, and the General Agreement on Tariff and Trade (GATT).

Bretton Woods became the birthplace of the US Dollar as a global reserve currency. Furthermore, USD was also established to be the only currency to have an actual equivalent of gold reserves.

As such, the US had to execute a series of balancing the deficit payments to make sure that the currency is the most stable in the world. However, in the 1970s, the US gold reserves were not sufficient to sustain the economic activities of the world.

In 1971, US Pres. Richard Nixon ended the Bretton Woods System by officially declaring the termination of the gold reserve system for the USD. In spite of the fact that the Bretton Woods system was a short-lived system, it still made an important contribution for the present-day world economy.

When the Bretton Woods disintegrated, world governments gradually embraced the floating rates for foreign exchange. But in 1976, the Jamaica Agreement led to the permanent elimination of the gold reserve standard. However, this didn't mean that government totally adopted the floating rate system. Many governments were still using floating rates, pegged rates, or dollar rates.

Floating Rates Mechanism

This exchange mechanism is established if the exchange rate of a currency is permitted to freely change in value according to the market forces of demand and supply. However, the central bank or the state could still interfere to ensure the stability of the currency if the exchange rates experience high fluctuation.

For instance, if the currency of a country is falling too much, the government may choose to increase short-term interest rates. This will in turn cause the currency to slightly appreciate. But take note that this is a macro perspective as central banks usually employ several tools for currency management.

Pegging refers to the practice of a country establishing a fixed exchange rate for another currency so that it becomes more stable compared to regular floating rates.

In particular, pegging will allow the currency of a country to have a fixed rate for the exchange with one or a specified group of foreign currencies. In addition, the currency may only fluctuate if there's a significant change in the pegged currencies.

In 1997 and 2005, the Chinese government pegged its currency to the US dollar at USD 1 to CNY 8.28. The disadvantage of pegging is that the value of the currency is now on the discretion of the economy of the country. For instance, when USD significantly increases its value against other denominations, the value of the Chinese yuan will also increase.

Dollarization

Dollarization happens if a country decides not to use its own currency and adopts the United States Dollars as its currency. Even though dollarization normally bestows a country with higher stability, the disadvantage is that the central bank of the country cannot make any form of monetary policy or print its own money.

Countries that adopted the US dollar include Zimbabwe, British Virgin Islands, Palau, Marshall Islands, El Salvador, East Timor, and Ecuador.

Chapter 2 - Forex Trading As A Business

"The expectation that you bring with you in trading is often the greatest obstacle you will encounter." — Yvan Byeajee

The forex market has boomed and it is now considered as one of the hottest financial markets today. It has been around for decades now, but the recent rise of trading technologies has made it accessible to private traders on a scale that is unprecedented.

At its core, forex trading is all about speculating the value of one currency against another. The key words in the preceding sentence are "currency" and "speculating". It is important to look at forex trading in these two dimensions.

First, forex trading is speculative similar to trading stocks or other financial instruments with the hope that it will increase its value and you as a trader will make a profit.

Second, the financial securities that you are speculating with are the currencies of different countries.

If we view these two dimensions separately, forex trading is both about the market speculation dynamics, as well as the factors that affect the value of currencies. If we combine these together, we get the biggest, most exciting financial market in the world.

In this book, we will see forex trading using these two perspectives, viewing them separately and integrating them to provide you the insights you need in order to trade successfully in the forex market.

Speculating as a Business

In general, speculating is all about taking risks in the hope of making money. However, it is neither investing nor gambling.

Investing is about reducing risk and maximizing returns, typically over an extended period of time.

Gambling is about playing with money even if you are not certain that you will win.

Speculating (also known as active trading) is about taking calculated risks to try making profits, normally over a very short time horizon.

In order to be a successful trader in any market (not just forex market) you need the following:

- Knowledge
- Decisiveness
- Perseverance

- Financial Resources

- Technological Resources

- Emotional Discipline

- Financial Discipline

- Dedication (Energy and Time)

But even if you possess all the traits listed above, there's no substitute for crafting a comprehensive trading plan. It can be foolish to open a business without first developing a plan. Therefore, you must not expect a resounding success in forex trading if you can't develop a realistic trading plan and follow it.

Consider forex trading as a business, and approach it as you would a real enterprise. Take it seriously. Moreover, you should not try to take the outcome of your trading too personally. Financial markets are susceptible to irrational movements, and the market doesn't care or know who you are and what you do. It will move even without you.

Currencies as Financial Instruments

You are probably aware that the forex market is the largest financial market in the world in terms of daily trading volumes. The forex market is also unique in many respects.

The liquidity is ever-present because of the huge volume in this market.

The forex market also operates 24 hours a day, six days a week, which can provide day traders with access to any market at any time. Furthermore, there are severe restrictions - no requirements in selling a currency pair short, no limits on the sizes of positions, and no daily trading limits.

When you are selling a pair in a short position, you are expecting for its price to fall. Because of the way currency pairs are quoted and because of the fluctuations in the forex market, short positions are quite as common as long positions in the market.

The majority of the action takes place in primary currency pairs that pit USD against Eurozone (countries in Europe that have adopted the euro as their currency), Switzerland, Great Britain, and Japan.

Plus, there's also a lot of trading opportunities in the minor currency pairs that see the USD traded against Australian Dollars (AUD), Canadian Dollars (CAD), and New Zealand Dollars (NZD). Then there's also the cross-currency trading that directly pits two non-USD currencies like Japanese Yen against Swiss Francs.

Depending on which forex brokerage you are dealing with, there are around 15 to 20 different major currency pairs.

Many individual traders are now trading currencies online (on a PC, tablet, or even mobile phone) but still through a brokerage firm.

Online forex trading is usually performed on a marginal basis that permits individual traders to trade huge amounts by leveraging the amount of margin on deposit. Trading with leverage is one of the key features of the forex market.

Also known as margin trading ratios, the leverage can be quite high, sometimes as high as 200:1 or even higher. In this leverage, a margin deposit of $1000 will allow you to control a position size of $200,000.

Trading with leverage is the backdrop against which all the trading will occur. It has its advantages, but it has its own requirements and rules as well. But you must remember that trading with leverage is like dealing with a two-edged sword. It can amplify your losses and gains that makes risk management the key to any lucrative trading strategy.

Before you begin trading in the forex market, you need to really understand your risk capital or the money you are willing to lose. Managing risk is the key to any successful trading plan.

Without a risk management-centric strategy, margin trading could be short-lived. With a proper risk plan in place, you stand a better chance of surviving losses in your trade and make money in the process.

The forex market is not affected by economic downturns as they do in other financial markets such as equities. Selling a currency pair is normal in this market, which is quite different in other financial markets. For instance, in the stock market, day traders don't usually sell stocks because of the financial risks involved.

Due to the fact that selling is quite common in currency market, it is virtually immune to financial downturns. Traders are always trading currency pairs, so something is always going up even in times of economic crisis.

Currency rates are primarily affected by information. Every financial market is driven by information, but the forex market has its own unique roster of information dynamics.

At any given moment, numerous cross-currencies are at play in the forex market. After all, the forex market is setting the value of one currency in relation to another currency.

Therefore, you are at least looking at information that is affecting two major economies of the world. Factor in other national economies, and you have a considerable information flowing through the market.

Market Fundamentals Driving the Forex Market

Fundamentals refer to the general grouping of information that reflects the political and macroeconomic conditions of the countries whose currencies are being traded.

More often than not, if you hear someone talking about currency fundamentals, he or she or referring to the economic fundamentals.

The basis of economic fundamentals are the following:

- Interest rate levels
- International trade flows
- Economic data reports
- Monetary policy
- International investment flows

Confidence or faith that the market is placing in the currency is an essential element of any currency's value. If political events like a political scandal, war, or a divisive election are perceived to undermine confidence in the leadership of a nation, the currency value could be affected negatively.

Gathering and making sense of this information will be part of your routine as a forex day trader.

Technical Drivers in the Forex Market

If you hear the word technicals in any financial markets, it usually means technical analysis, which is a method of analyzing a market that involves trend-line analysis, chart analysis, and mathematical studies of price behavior like moving averages or momentum trading.

Technical analysis is also crucial in forex trading so don't ignore the technicals. If you are also engaged in other financial markets, there's a big chance that you already worked with technical analysis. If you want to actively trade in the forex market, then you need to familiarize yourself with the basics.

Don't be intimidated by the name. Technical analysis is just like a tool that you can use to complete a job similar to a cellphone. You don't have to understand the whole mechanism of a cellphone before you learn how to use it. However, you need to know how to use it properly so you can use it to call someone, send a text message, or use mobile applications.

Technical analysis is crucial in currency trading because of the amount of fundamental data hitting the market at any point in time. Forex market traders regularly apply different forms of technical analysis in order to define and refine their trading strategies with a lot of traders trading currency pairs based on technical indicators.

Take note that forex trading is just one type of market speculation, and speculative trading involves inherent dynamics in the market.

The forex market is composed of hundreds of thousands of various traders with different perspectives of the market and each expressing his view by either selling or buying various currencies at different times and price points.

So on top of understanding the specific fundamentals of a currency and getting to know technical indicators, you also need to really appreciate market dynamics (also known as market psychology or sentiment). This is where trading with a plan comes in.

The Importance of a Trading Plan

It is important first to settle your trading style before you start developing your forex trading plan. Various trading styles basically call for variations on trading plans, even though there are a lot of overarching rules in trading that are applicable to all styles.

Trading style all boils down to how you approach currency trading in terms of the following:

Time Frame

You need to determine how long you would hold your position. Some forex traders look at short-term trade opportunities. This is known as day trading. Meanwhile, some traders are trying to capture more significant movements in forex prices over days, weeks or even months.

Currency Pair

Are you looking to trade in different currency pairs or are you more interested to focus your energy into few pairs?

Risk Appetite

How much money are you willing to risk and what is your level of expectations for your trading profits?

Rationale

Are you technically or fundamentally inclined? Are you looking to develop a systematic trading model? What strategies are you looking to follow? Are you comfortable in following forex trends? Or are you more inclined to become a breakout forex trader?

Don't worry if you still don't have answers to these questions.

Hopefully as you read this book, you can choose the forex trading approach you are interested to pursue.

You can try different strategies and styles by using demo accounts. But don't forget that your goal is to zero in your

trading style that you feel comfortable with and that you can pursue regularly.

In addition, you also need to consider other factors such as your individual circumstances such as personal discipline, temperament, finances, free time, family, and work obligations. These are essential variables and you are the only one who knows how they impact your forex trading.

Regardless of the trading style you choose to pursue, achieving success can be challenging if you don't set your

trade plan then follow it. Remember, trade plans will help you avoid losing a lot of money from bad trades and can also help you win big in the market.

Moreover, your trading plan serves as your guide, which helps you explore the trades after the emotions and adrenaline begin pumping regardless of what the market presents to you. But this doesn't mean that forex trading is

any easier compared to other financial markets.

However, it is proven that trading with a plan will significantly improve the probability of your success in the forex market over time. Also, you need to understand that trading without a plan is a guaranteed way to lose money in the forex market.

Sure, you may make money from a few trades, but a day of reckoning will eventually come to any trader who is only guided by his guts. This is always the trend in any financial markets.

The starting line of any trading plan is to determine an opportunity for trading. Do not wait for any writing on the wall that will tell you what and when to trade. You must devote your effort and energy in looking for lucrative opportunities for trading. In this book, you will learn some expert insights on forex market behavior in different settings.

Trading Plan Execution

Forex trading begins once you step into the market and you open a position. The way you approach this initial step is as important as the trade opportunity itself. Remember, if you have never enter the position, you will not be able to exploit any trade opportunity.

And possibly, nothing is more disappointing as a trader than identifying a trade opportunity, having it to go the way you are expecting, but you can't reap the results because you have never opened a position in the first place.

The money and energy you invest in studying, tracking, and assessing the forex market comes to a solid outcome only if you open a trade. This process is a lot easier by developing your own trading system with setups and trigger points that can help you in entering the trade.

Placing the trade is just the start. The mere fact of owning a trading plan doesn't mean that the market will keep on

rolling. You must actively engage in managing your position in order to maximize it if the position is a winner then reduce the damage if the market is going against your expectations.

In order to retain most of your earnings, you should have an active trade management plan in place. With the right strategy and discipline, it can be easy to earn money in currency trading. The real challenge comes in maintaining your profits.

It is crucial that you learn how to keep yourself on the ground. The forex market will always move, usually a lot quicker than usual. Moreover, new information will be coming into the market. Later in this book, we will look at various ways that you can keep track of your active trades and also how and when you must adjust your trade strategy depending on time and events.

Trade exits serve as the finale of the whole process, where you can either make money or lose money unless of course you exit at the entry price. This is just the way the market works.

Even though your trade is still active, you should take note that you are still in control and you may choose to exit the trade at any time. We'll take a look at important tactical considerations that you need to bear in mind when it is time to close the trade.

Your trade is still not complete even after you have exited the position. If you really want to treat forex trading as a serious business, you must reassess your immediate past trades so you can obtain a more general perspective about recent trends and method of execution.

One way to focus on your trades is to document your trading history. Carefully study your previous trading style so you can gain insights on strategies that are effective.

Chapter 3 – The Forex Market

"The goal of a successful trader is to make the best trades. Money is secondary." -
Alexander Elder

The foreign exchange market (commonly known simply as the forex market, or just FX market) is the biggest and most liquid of all financial markets around the world.

This financial market is the crossroads for global capital, the intersection via which worldwide investment and commercial flows are dynamic.

Global trade flows such as if a South Korean company buys French-made furniture, were the original basis for the development of these markets. But today, global financial flows dominate trade as the main non-speculative source for market volume.

Whether it's a Canadian pension fund investing in Australian

Treasury bonds or a Swiss insurer allocating assets to the stock markets in Hong Kong, or a Japanese conglomerate buying a Brazilian manufacturing plant, each international transaction has to pass through the forex market at some stage. As such, the forex market is considered as the ultimate market for traders.

The forex market is open 24 hours a day and six days a week. This enables traders to quickly act on events and news as they happen. This is the trading platform where $500 million trades can easily be completed in a few seconds and may not even affect the whole market. This is one unique trait in the forex market. Try selling or buying units in other markets and it will be chaotic.

Organizations like IG Group, CMC Markets, Oanda, Saxo Bank, and Forex.com have made the FX market accessible to retail traders. This allows you to trade the same forex units with hedge funds and big financial conglomerates.

Trillion Dollar Market Volume

The average daily forex trading volumes in the forex market exceeds $5 trillion daily. Now, that's a lot of money. To provide you some idea on this volume, this is around 10 times the everyday trading volume of the stock markets around the world combined.

And remember, that volume is daily!

But take note that this high daily trading volume that you might have seen in newspapers or in other books on forex trading, actually overstates the size of what the foreign exchange market is really about - spot forex trading.

Spot Forex Trading

"Spot" pertains to the rate where you can trade currencies at the moment. Bear in mind that in the equities market, the rates that you can trade is basically a spot rate. This term is basically used to identify the difference between a spot or cash trading from futures trading, in which the delivery date of the units are settled on a future date.

The spot forex market is settled in two trading days. Unless explicitly written in a contract, the spot rate is more likely what you trade with your forex broker.

Forex Market Speculation

Even though financial and commercial transactions in the forex markets represent significant nominal sums, they still fade in comparison to the amounts based on speculation.

At this point, the huge majority of forex trading volume is based on speculation - traders buy and sell for short-term gains based on hourly and daily fluctuations.

Forex trading experts estimate that upwards of 90% of daily trading volume is derived from speculation, which means commercial or investment-based forex trades account for less than 10% of daily global volume.

The breadth and depth of the speculative market means that the liquidity of the general forex market is unparalleled among worldwide financial markets.

The majority of spot forex trading, around 75% by volume, happens with primary currencies that represent the largest economies of the world. Trading primary currencies is significantly free from government regulation and happens outside the authority of any national or international organization.

Moreover, the movement in the forex market regularly functions on a regional bloc basis where the majority of trading happens between the EUR bloc, JPY bloc, and USD bloc signifying the biggest global economic blocs of the world.

Trading in currencies used by developing nations like the Philippines or Argentina, is usually referred to as exotic forex trading or emerging market. While trading in emerging markets has significantly grown in recent years, in terms of volume, it still remains the same way behind major currencies.

Because of some internal catalysts (like local restrictions on forex transactions) and some external catalysts (like geopolitical crises and the crash of financial markets making the emerging market challenging to trade) the emerging market is significantly less liquid that can turn off small investors.

Always Be Mindful of Liquidity

Liquidity pertains to the market interest and trading volume available at any point in time for a particular financial instrument. The higher the liquidity or the deeper the market, the faster and easier it is to buy or sell an instrument.

As a forex trader, you need to always be mindful of liquidity because this will allow you to figure out how fast the currency prices will move between your trades. Remember, the forex market has high liquidity so you will usually experience huge trading volumes but with minor price changes.

The market is called a thin market or illiquid if its price moves a lot faster on relatively lower trading volumes. In comparison, a stock market has medium-level of liquidity because it only trades during specific hours.

Take note that in this guide, we will always refer to liquidity because this is one of the most important factors that can affect price action and movement. Even though the forex market has high liquidity, the volume may vary throughout the trading day and across different currencies.

For forex day traders, variations in liquidity yearns more on strategy rather than tactics.

If a hedge fund company requires millions of a particular company, its analysts will first look on the tactical side of liquidity such as how much the trade will cause price fluctuations depending on the performance of the trade and its time.

But for day traders who generally trade in smaller units, the trade size is not a major concern. The strategic liquidity level is an important factor in timing of when and how prices are most likely to behave.

Throughout this book, we will take a closer look on fluctuations on liquidty and market interest with a special lens relevant to trading in particular forex pairs.

Trading Day Around the World

The foreign exchange market is active 24 hours daily from the beginning of business hours on Monday morning in Asia straight through end of business hours in New York. At any point in time, depending on the time zone, leading financial centers such as London, Tokyo, or Sydney, are active and open.

Aside from leading financial centers around the world, numerous financial organizations also operate 24 hours a day. This provides an ever-present source of market interest. Forex trading centers are even active during holidays when other markets such as futures or stocks are closed.

While it's a holiday in Sydney, for example, Hong Kong, or Singapore may still be active. It might be National Founding

Day in Japan, but if it's a business day, Toronto, London, and New York and other financial centers are still trading currencies. New Year's Day is probably the only holiday common around the world, and even that depends on the day it falls on.

Opening of Trades

There's no official starting time for forex trading, but the market is active when Wellington, New Zealand starts on Monday morning. This is around Sunday afternoon in North America, Monday morning in Asia, or Sunday night in Europe. (Note: This still depends if Daylight Savings Time or DST is active in your time zone.)

Take for example the Sunday open, which signifies the beginning where forex markets trade again after trade closes in North America on Friday. This is 5 in the afternoon Eastern Time. This is the first opportunity for the forex market to react to news and events that could have happened over the weekend.

Prices may have closed Tokyo trading at one level, but depending on current events, they may begin trading at various levels at the opening on Sunday. Weekend gap risk or

Sunday open gap risk refers to the risk that the forex rates open at different levels on Sunday versus Friday close.

The gap refers to the price level movements where prices are unable to trade in between. As a retail trader, you should understand the Sunday gap risk and know what events are expected to happen over the weekend.

There's no guaranteed set of political events and there's no

way to rule out what could transpire such as a natural disaster, a geopolitical conflict or a terror attack. You just need to be conscious about the existence of risks and consider it into your forex trading strategy.

Of the usual pre-determined events over the weekend, the most typical are the national referenda or elections or the quarterly G20 meetings. Make certain that you are aware of any major events that are scheduled. For example, during the height of the debt crisis in Europe, numerous last-minute bailout decisions were decided over the weekend. These developments have major implications for the financial markets when they opened.

On a typical Sunday opens, prices basically pick up where they left off on Friday afternoon. The price spreads in the opening of the interbank market will be much wider than the usual because only New Zealand and 24-hour trading desks are active in this period.

The opening price spreads of 10-30 points in the primary currency pairs are not uncommon during the early trading hours. Once banks in Australia and Asia centers enter the forex market over the next few hours, market liquidity starts to improve and the price spreads start to narrow to more regular levels.

Because of the wider price spreads during the early hours of Sunday open, many online trading platforms don't start trading until 5 pm Eastern Time on Sundays. During this period, the liquidity enables the platforms to offer their regular price quotes.

With these things in mind, it is crucial that you are aware of the trading policies of your brokers in connection with the Sunday open, particularly in terms of trading executions.

Asia-Pacific Trading Session

According to the survey results released by BIS in 2014, the trading volumes of the forex markets in Asia Pacific accounts for around 21 per cent of the average global volume. The largest financial trading centers in this region are Wellington (New Zealand), Tokyo (Japan), Hong Kong, Sydney (Australia), and Singapore.

News announcements from Japan, Australia and New Zealand shall hit the forex world in the first session.

Australia and New Zealand reports are regularly issued in the early morning local time, which is roughly mid-morning in the US Eastern Time.

News announcements from Japan are usually issued before the 9 am session in Tokyo, which is roughly around 7 pm in the US Eastern Time.

In some trading days, important Japanese reports are issued in the afternoon, which is roughly around 4 am US Eastern time. The whole trading movement for the NZD, AUD, and JPY can be set for the whole trading session, depending on the the substance of the news reports and what they mean for the market.

Moreover, news reports from China mainly about Asian economy, interest rate changes, comments from political leaders, and policy changes can also affect the market.

In some days, American sources of information such as the Federal Reserve can also affect the other regions such as when an official issue a controversial comment on the US economy or if the interest rates in the US suddenly changes.

Because of the sheer size of the Japanese market as well as the significance of the Japanese current events, majority of the action in this trading region revolves around currency pairs that involve JPY such as EUR/JPY, AUD/JPY and of course USD/JPY.

Japanese companies and financial firms are also active in their own time zone so you should watch out from these sources if you have interest in JPY currency pairs.

For forex day traders, the general liquidity in major forex pairs is enough to predict the price movements. In less liquid, non-regional currencies like GBP/USD or USD/CAD, the price movements may be erratic or even non-existent depending on the market environment.

With few reports from Canada issued for the next half-day session, there could be limited interest or reason for this pair to move. But if an important market player has the need to start a transaction in this pair, the price movement can be bigger than normal.

European Trading Session

European trading centers begin to open around the middle of the Asian session. At this time, the market is in full swing. These financial organizations, especially London (United Kingdom) contributes more than half of the global total trading volume. UK alone comprises about 30% of the global average volume (BIS survey, 2014).

The European trading session overlaps with half of the trading day in Asia and also 50% of the North American trading session. Thus, the market interest as well as the liquidity is at its highest peak in this specific time window.

News announcements from Europe (as well as countries like UK, Germany, France, and Switzerland) are typically issued in the early morning hours of Eurozone trading.

Hence, some of the most important price movements and trading fluctuations occur in currencies from this region such as GBP, CHF and EUR. This includes cross-currency pairs in Europe such as EUR/CHF and EUR/GBP.

The Asian trading session begins to dwindle down roughly around mid-day in Europe and North American financial centers open several hours later around 7 am US Eastern Time.

North American Trading Session

Due to the overlap of the trading sessions in North America and Europe, you should always be mindful of the trading volumes in these specific time zones. Some of the biggest and most important price movements happen during the crossover between the trading sessions of these two regions.

The trading volume in North America accounts for around the same percentage of Asia Pacific that is roughly 25% of the daily trading volume.

The trading session in North America starts when important economic information in the US are released. Remember, key decisions in the forex market mainly involve the USD.

Most data reports coming from this region are released at 8:30 US Eastern Time with other financial centers issued later in the day not later than 10 am. Some financial reports in the US are released at various times at mid-day or not later than 2 pm. This activated the New York forex market in the afternoon. European centers begin to wind down the daily trading sessions around noontime.

There is also volatility when the European trading closes down. A significant trend that occurred before early afternoon in Europe or in New York can still be reversed if sufficient volume of trades happen to cover shorts or take profit.

An overwhelming trend can also further extend as more traders are trying to jump on board prior to the closing of the trading session. Take note that there's no fixed formula that the European trading follows in the closing session. But it is almost predictable that considerably volatility in the market occurs around this time.

On regular trading sessions, liquidity dwindles down in the afternoon session in New York. This can be a bit of a challenge for day traders. On more "peaceful" days, the usually lower liquidity often results to sustained price action.

On more active days when prices usually move around, the lower liquidity could add more price movements because few traders are pursuing better liquidity and better currency prices.

Like the European close there's no fixed method in which the North American session will play out the movements. Therefore, you must be aware that lower liquidity conditions have a high tendency to prevail and adapt accordingly.

Higher volatility and a chance for lower liquidity is more apparent in the low-liquid major pairs especially GBP/USD and USD/CHF.

Trading volume and interest in the North American region basically continue to dwindle down as the trading day moves toward later afternoon session in New York. This is also the time, which sudden changes usually occur. But the new trading session begins as Wellington and Sydney opens in the afternoon in North America.

London is considered as the center of the forex market world. But there's a lot of opportunities if you take advantage of the salient moments in the North American and Asian sessions.

As a forex trader, you must remember that if you are trading in Asia, and there's no significant news announcement, the trend caused by the North American session prior to today's trading usually prevails.

Important Daily Times and Events

Aside from the market interest and liquidity movement during worldwide forex trading day, you also need to be aware of key daily events that tend to happen around the same time every day.

Options Expiry

Currency options are usually set to expire either at the New York expiry (10 a.m. Eastern Time) or the Tokyo expiry (3 p.m. Tokyo time). The option expiry in New York is the more important expiry option since it has the tendency to capture both North American and European option market interest. Once an option expires, the underlying option stops to exist.

Remember, any spot market hedging done based on the option being suddenly alive should be carefully monitored. This triggers important price changes in the hours leading up to and just after the expiry time of the option.

The variety and the amount of currency option interest is just too big to suggest any one method to spot the prices. However, if you are getting some volatility around 10 am Eastern Time, this could be caused by the expiry of some currency options.

Establishing the Rate at Currency Fixtures

Currency fixing refers to a set time every day when the prices of currencies for business transactions are fixed or set.

There are scheduled currency fixtures in different financial centers around the world. However, the two most important are the London Time (4 p.m.) and the Tokyo Time (8:55 a.m.).

From a trading perspective, these fixtures may see a surge in a specific currency pair (usually 15 to 30 minutes) to the fixing time that suddenly ends precisely.

A sharp movement in a particular currency pair on fixing-related buying, for instance, may suddenly come to an end at the fixing time and see the price immediately drop back to where it was before.

Traditionally, the London Forex Fix is benchmarked to WM/ Reuters fixing rates.

Squaring Up on the Forex Futures Markets

One of the biggest futures markets in the world, the Chicago Mercantile Exchange (CME), offers forex futures through the International Monetary Market

(IMM) subsidiary exchange. A forex futures contract specifies at which a specific currency can be purchased or sold in the future.

The trading of currency futures closes every day on the IMM at 2 p.m. central time (CT) or around 3 pm in the East Coast. Numerous traders in the futures market usually square up or close any open positions at the end of every trading session for margin requirements or to limit their exposure overnight. The last hour leading to the closing of the IMM usually creates a surge that spills over into the spot market.

Market liquidity is usually at the lowest in the afternoon in New York. This results in sharp movements in the futures market that can trigger volatility in the spot market around this period.

There's no easy way to tell if or how the IMM close will cause a movement in the spot market in New York, so you have to be aware of this.

The USD Index

The USD index is a futures contract that is listed in the New York Board of Trade (NYBOT) and Financial Instruments Exchange (FINEX) futures exchanges that is based in Dublin.

The dollar index refers to the average USD value against a basket of six other primary currencies. However, this is heavily weighted towards currencies in Europe.

Here are the specific weights of other currencies in the USD index:

- Swiss Franc (3.6%)

- Swedish Krona (4.2%)

- Canadian Dollar (9.1%)

- British Pound (11.9%)

- Japanese Yen (13.6%)

- Euro (57.6%)

Take note that the European currency share of the basket (Switzerland, Sweden, United Kingdom, and Eurozone) accounts for 77.3%.

USD is the most powerful currency today with the majority of forex trading normally involving the dollar on one side of the pair. Global commodities are valued in USD and numerous global currency reserves maintained by central banks are in USD.

It is not surprising that the USD is considered as the most liquid currency in the world.

As a day trader, you need to know if the USD is strong or weak. The USD index allows you to do this because it provides you a wider perspective of how the dollar is performing in the G10 forex space. As a forex trader, you should follow the USD index especially its technical developments.

Forex and Other Financial Instruments

While forex market is the largest financial market in the world in terms of daily trading volume, it is not the only financial instrument that you can trade. Aside from currencies, you can also trade gold, oil, and of course company equities or stocks.

You have probably heard about the supposed interconnectivity of forex to these financial instruments. Unfortunately, much of the information out there are not true at all and you should learn how to determine which one is true and which one is just pure hype.

Seasoned forex traders usually look for a link between two different financial instruments depending on individual circumstances. You must be careful in getting caught up in these "connections".

Even if there's an apparent connection between two instruments (moving in harmony or inversely against each other) it usually happens over the long term - months or even years. This connection usually provides minimal information on how the markets will connect in the short term, which is an important factor to consider if you are a forex day trader.

And even if two instruments are connected with each other in the short-term, there's no certainty if the correlation will persist in the long-term.

For example, depending on where you look at the performance of gold and USD (inverse connection) you may still find a correlation co-efficient (not less than -0.2 and not more than -0.8). Remember, if you see a zero correlation in the charts, it means that the two instruments are not correlated at all.

Different financial instruments are traded in their own markets, so they behave in their own internal dynamics based on the market interest, trader positions, and significance of news.

There's a possibility that the financial markets might overlap and will demonstrate various degrees of correlation. And as a trader, it will help you if you are also aware of what is happening in other financial markets.

But you should look at each market in its own right and to have your own strategy and trading plan for each instrument.

For now, we can briefly discuss other important financial instruments and see their correlation with currencies.

Stocks

Stocks refer to the units of shares in the equities market. The movement in the stock market follow individual prospects for each company, sector or industry that you hold shares.

On the other hand, currencies are much larger securities that usually fluctuate in response to various economic and political developments.

Hence, there's minimal logic that the stock market is correlated to the forex market. Long-term correlation studies bear this out with the co-efficient of 0 between the main USD pairs and the stock markets.

There are some instances that the currencies and stocks cross each other, even though this is rare and for short-term only.

For example, when the equity market volatility peaks on (such as when S&P 500 loses higher than 2 per cent in a single trading day) the USD can also experience more tension than the usual. However, there's no way to predict this through correlation studies.

NASDAQ may dwindle down during an unexpected rise in interest rates, while the USD may even increase on the sudden surge.

Meanwhile, the Japanese stock market can be affected by JPY value mainly because of the significance of the export sector in the Japanese economy.

A sudden rise in the value of JPY may cause a negative response in the equities market because this would make exports more expensive and thus could affect the value of import sales.

Fixed Income Markets

Fixed income markets mainly trade bonds, wherein you are guaranteed an income within a specific time. The bond market has a more intuitive correlation to currencies compared to equities because the bonds and currencies are both significantly affected by interest rate movements.

However, the short-term market dynamics of supply and demand usually affects the efforts to establish a possible correlation between the two instruments for short-term.

In some instances, the forex market could respond first based on the changes in interest rate movements. There are times that the bond market could reflect the changes in the expectations on the interest rate with the currencies trying to follow.

If you want to become a forex day trader, you should look at the current yields of government bonds on major currencies so you can monitor the possible changes in interest rates.

Gold

In Chapter 1, we have learned that gold was used by governments to back up the value of their currencies. While this is no longer the case today, gold is still used by investors and traders as a hedge against inflation and it is also a much more valuable alternative to the USD.

For long term, the correlation between gold and USD is typically inverse. If the dollar is weaker, then gold is stronger. If the dollar is stronger, then gold is weaker.

But for short term, the two markets have their own interest level and liquidity that makes the correlation between them too tedious.

Basically, the gold market is a lot smaller compared to the currencies. Thus, if you are also interested in trading gold, you should also monitor the movement of USD.

Robust movements in the price of gold can attract the attention of forex traders and typically affect the dollar inversely.

Oil

Some financial experts say that there's a correlation between oil and currencies especially JPY and USD. This is basically based on the premise that because some countries are oil-producing countries, their currencies are influenced by the oil price.

The assumption is, if a country is importing oil, then its currency is affected by the oil price fluctuations.

However, correlation studies show no clear link to back this up, especially in the short-term. If there's a correlation in the long-term, this is usually against the USD as much as more than any currency regardless if the country is importing or exporting oil.

Take note that oil is seen as an input to calculate inflation and also considered as a factor that can limit the general growth of a country's economy.

Higher oil price may lead to higher inflation rate and the other way around. Because of the fact that the US is significantly reliant on energy, and also heavily driven by capitalism, it favors lower oil prices.

If you also want to speculate in the oil market while trading currencies, you need to consider the fluctuation in the oil prices when you look at growth projections and inflation of a certain country.

But remember, there are other factors that affect the overall financial markets, not only oil price.

Chapter 4 – How Forex Trading Works

"You don't need to be a rocket scientist. Investing is not a game where the guy with the 160 IQ beats the guy with 130 IQ." - Warren Buffett

Just like any other financial market, the forex market also has its own trading norms and jargon.

If you are new to forex trading, you may need some time to learn the terminology and mechanics of the market. But basically, you will see that most forex norms are quite straightforward and easy to understand.

One of the largest mental obstacles facing newbies to forex trading is really understanding the concept that every trade in the forex is composed of buying and selling.

For example in the equities market, if you purchase 200 shares of Amazon, it is clear that you now own 200 shares and you hope that the share price will increase. If you like to exit this position, all you have to do is to sell all your shares or a percentage of it.

But in the case of forex trading, we need to understand the concept of exchange. If you are looking for USD to go up, you need another currency for the benchmark.

If USD is stronger against another currency, it also means that the other currency will go down against USD. Viewing this in the language of equities market, you are actually selling money. Remember, if you are selling shares, you are buying money.

Currency Pairs

To put it simply, the currency market refers to trading two different currencies. Currency pairs have abbreviations or nicknames that refer to the pair but does not necessarily involve the individual currencies.

The USD is the main currency against which other currencies are traded in the forex market. According to the Bank of International Settlements (BIS), USD is involved in 87% of all reported transactions in the forex market. Its position as the dominant currency has remained virtually unopposed for more than five decades.

The central role of USD in the forex market is rooted from several fundamental factors:

- USA is the largest economy in the world

- USA has the biggest and most liquid financial markets in the world

- USA is a global military superpower with stable political climate

Countries	ISO Currency Pair	Conventional Name	Market Nickname
United States and Japan	USD/JPY	Dollar-Yen	None
Eurozone and United States	EUR/USD	Euro-Dollar	None
New Zealand and United States	NZD/USD	New Zealand-Dollar	Kiwi
Australia and United States	AUD/USD	Australian-Dollar	Oz or Aussie
United States and Canada	USD/CAD	Dollar-Canada	Loonie
United States and Switzerland	USD/CHF	Dollar-Swiss	Swissy

United Kingdom and United States	GBP/USD	Pound-Dollar	Cable or Sterling

As a result, USD is now the main international reserve currency and it is also used for numerous international transactions. For instance, oil is priced in USD. So even if you are a Chinese oil importer buying crude from Saudi Arabia, you need USD to settle the transaction.

Major Currency Pairs

USD is involved in all major currency pairs with designations expressed using the codes established by the International Standardization Organization (ISO) for every currency.

The table below shows the commonly used currency pairs with their traditional names and market nicknames.

Note: Eurozone is composed of all member countries of the European Union that have adopted the Euro as their currency. This includes Austria, Spain, Belgium, Slovenia, Cyprus, Portugal, Estonia, the Netherlands, Finland, Malta, France, Luxembourg, France, Italy, Germany, Ireland, and Greece.

Some newbies are confused over currency names and nicknames when they read market commentaries or following the market in general. To avoid confusion, you need to understand if the forex analyst or writer is referring to the currency pair or the individual currency.

For example, if an analyst is discussing a study suggesting that Australian Dollars is expected to be weaker the next few months, the discussion refers to the currency itself (AUD in this case) expecting that USD/AUD will go upwards (USD is strong and AUD is weak).

But when the analysis suggests that Aussie is expected to be weaker in the immediate future, it now refers to the currency pair, which indicates a forecast that USD/AUD will go downwards (USD weak / AUD strong).

Primary Cross Currency Pairs

While the bulk of forex trading happens with USD, cross currency pairs provide an alternative way to trade forex.

Basically, cross-currency pair (simply crosses or cross) refers to any pair, which doesn't involve the USD.

The rates for crosses originate from their corresponding USD pairs but independently quoted and normally with a lower spread compared to what you can obtain from directly trading USD.

Take note that the "spread" pertains to the difference between the offer and the bid or the rate at which you could trade. You will encounter the spread in almost all finance markets.

Cross currencies allow traders to directly move target trades to particular individual currencies to take advantage of important events or news.

For instance, forecast suggests that CAD has the lowest prospects of all major currencies to go forward, based on economic outlook or interest rates. You may take advantage of this by selling CAD. But to what pair?

You may consider the USD, possibly buying USD/CAD (buying USD and selling CAD). However, you think that the prospects of USD are not much better than CAD. After taking a closer look, you identified a currency that has a much better outlook (such as strengthening economy or rising interest rates), say the New Zealand Dollar (NZD).

In this case, we are looking to buy CAD/NZD cross (buying CAD and selling NZD) to take advantage of your projection that the NZD has the best potential among major currencies and CAD the worst.

Cross trading can be particularly effective if major cross-border mergers and acquisitions (M&A) are released. If a Japanese conglomerate is buying an Australian software company, the Japanese company needs to sell JPY and buy AUD to fund the acquisition.

For M&As, you need to watch out for the cash portion of the transaction. If the transaction involves stocks, then there is no need to exchange currencies to raise the needed cash.

The three major non-USD currencies (GBP, JPY, and EUR) are presently the most actively traded cross currencies. These are known as the sterling crosses, yen crosses, and euro crosses. The rest of the currencies (NZD, CAD, AUD, and CHF) are also traded in cross pairs.

Base Currencies and Counter Currencies

If you study the currency pairs, you may realize that the currencies are combined in a seemingly peculiar order. For example if Aussie-yen (AUD/JPY) is a yen cross, then why is this not called a "yen-Aussie" and written JPY/AUD?

The quoting norms evolved over the years to follow conventionally strong currencies as opposed to traditionally weak currencies, with the strong currency coming first. It also reflects the norm in market quotations where the first currency in the pair is called the base currency.

The base currency refers to what you are buying or selling when you are trading the pair. This is also called notional or face amount of the trade. Therefore, if you buy 50,000 GBP/AUD, you have just purchased 50,000 pounds and sold the equal amount in Australian Dollars. If you sell 50,000

CAD/GBP, you just sold 50,000 Canadian Dollars and purchased the equivalent amount of British Pounds.

The counter currency refers to the second currency in the pair. As such, it is also known as the secondary currency. It also refers to the denomination of the price fluctuations and ultimately what you earn and lose will be denominated in the counter currency. If you buy CHF/AUD, it goes up and you take a profit, your gains are not in francs but in Aussie.

Long, Short and Flat

Like other financial markets, the forex market also uses the same names in discussing market positioning. But due to the fact that forex trading involves trading currencies at the same time, you need to be really accurate on the contextual definition of these terms, especially if you are a newbie.

Long Position

Long position refers to a trade position wherein you are buying a unit of security. In the forex market, this refers to buying a currency pair. If you are long, it means you are searching for rates to move higher, so you may sell it at a better price compared to when you purchased the security.

If you want to close a long position, you are interested to sell what you have purchased. If you are purchasing at different price levels, you are sustaining longs so your position is "getting longer".

Short Position

Short position refers to selling units that you never owned in the first place. In equities, shorting a stock refers to borrowing the stock so you can resell the units (less the broker fees).

In the forex market, this refers to the actual trading of two currencies, which means you are selling the "base" and buying the "counter". Therefore, the exchange is still present, but just in reverse order and in reference to the quoting terms for currency pairs.

Once you have sold a currency pair, it is now called getting short, which means you are now searching for lower rates so you can buy it back and then make profits from the difference.

When you are selling at different price levels, you are going for shorts and so your position is getting "shorter". In other financial markets, short selling are bounded by certain restrictions and usually considered too risky for many day traders. But in forex trading, getting short is quite common as getting long.

"Sell high and buy low" is a common mantra in financial markets. But take note that the forex pair prices are not absolute because they only indicate the relative values between the two currencies.

Due to the fact that currencies may rise or fall relevant to each other in long-term and medium trends, and short-term market activities, currency pair rates can easily go down or up.

In order to leverage this activity, forex traders usually go short to take advantage of declining currency rates. Players from other financial markets may find it risky to short sell. However, this is just something that you need to embrace.

Flat Position

When you are in a flat position, it means you have no position in the market. It also called a square position. If you are currently in short, you need to buy currencies so you can "square up". When you are long, then you need to sell currencies so you can go "flat". A square position generally carries no financial risk or exposure.

NOTE: The only time that you don't have financial risk or exposure is when you are square.

Profit and Loss

Seasoned traders in any financial market are trained in analyzing Profit and Loss (P&L) reports to ascertain if they are winning or losing the trade. Bear in mind that these financial markets are not theoretical or academic. You can earn or lose a lot of money within minutes. If you want to actively trade currencies, you have to really master P&L.

Understanding the mechanism behind P&L is crucial, especially if you are interested in online marketing trading. In this case, your P&L will directly affect the margin level you need to recover.

The slight movements in your margin account will help you figure out how much you can buy and sell and also the duration of the trade if the rates are not looking good for your current position.

Liquidations and Margin Balances

One of the key advantages of forex trading is that you can use the leverage that will enable you to obtain a bigger exposure to a market while only using a small percentage of your capital.

Margin refers to the initial capital that you have to post in your trading account in order to start trading. This margin will now become your starting balance. This now becomes the basis on which all your trades will be used as collateral. This is similar to a collateral that a bank will ask you before approving a loan.

Not similar to margin-based stock trading or futures market, online forex brokers don't usually issue requests for more leverage so you can sustain more open positions. As an alternative, they establish margin ratios to open positions, which should be sustained regularly.

If the margin balance of your account falls below the needed ratio even for just a few moments, your broker may close out your positions without any prior notice.

This usually happens if your account is currently in a losing position. When your broker liquidates your positions, you are most likely tied in and the size of your margin balance can be reduced.

Make certain that you are totally aware of your broker's requirements for leverage and policies for liquidation. The requirements may vary depending on the size of your account.

Some brokers may liquidate your trading account when you go under the margin limits. Other brokers, on the other hand, may just close out your largest losing trades until you can fulfill the recommended ratio again. Please go over the terms and conditions relevant to leverage and liquidation before you sign up.

Market-to-Market Computations

Many online brokers will provide you actual market-to-market computations, which will show your account's margin balance. This computation will show your profit and loss (unrealized) according to the exact moment that you can close your positions in the trade.

Depending on the trading platform used by your broker, if you are long, the computation will use the exact moment that you can sell as the basis. If your position is short, the rate will be based on the exact moment you can buy.

On the other hand, margin balance refers to the total amount you have deposited initially, as well as your P&L (both realized and unrealized).

Once you go flat (close all open positions at full), all of your earnings will be diverted to your margin balance. If you partially close some of your positions, only the corresponding percentage of your P&L shall be realized and will be diverted to your margins.

The unrealized P&L shall continue to fluctuate based on the remaining open positions and so will your total margin balance. If you have a winning position open, you'll have a positive unrealized P&L and your broker may increase your margin balance.

When the market is moving against the positions the unrealized P&L will be negative and your broker may reduce the size of your margin balance. Take note that the prices in the forex market are always changing, so your total margin balance and market-to-market unrealized P&L will also change.

Using Pips to Calculate Profit and Loss

The computations for P&L are quite mathematically direct. Forex analysts only use the pips you have lost or gained and the size of your position as bases.

Pip refers to the basic increase of price changes on the prevailing rates of a currency. Pips are also referred to as points, so you may find these terms used interchangeably.

It's not certain where the word pip came from. Some say this

is an abbreviation for percentage in point, but it may also refer to the FX response to the bips or bond traders that refer to the bps or basis points.

Even the conventionally strong pip is now being updated as electronic trading continues to develop. It is true that a pip is the smallest increment of fluctuations in the currency price rates.

However, you should take note that online forex trading is rapidly progressing to use decimals in pips, wherein you can trade 1/10 pips. Furthermore, half-pip prices have been the norm in specific currency pairs in the interbank market for several years. But as a newbie, it is ideal that you stick with pips for now.

Now, let's take a look at several currency pairs so you can get an idea of what a pip is. Many currency pairs are quoted in five digits. The position of the decimal points depends on whether it's a yen currency pair - if it is, there are two digits after the decimal point.

For the rest of the currency pairs, there are 4 digits after the decimal point. In all cases, the pip is reflected in the last digit. Below are some of the major currency pairs and crosses. Take note that the underlined digits are the pips.

- USD/JPY: 101.4**3**
- USD/CHF: 0.907**4**
- EUR/USD: 1.353**5**
- EUR/JPY: 138.0**1**
- GBP/USD: 1.614**2**

Take a look at GBP/USD. In this case, if the rate increases from 1.6142 to 1.16162, it has increased by 20 units. When the rate moves from 1.6142 to 1.6122, it just went down by 20 pips. Pips offer an easy way to compute the P&L. To turn the movement of the pip into a P&L computation, all you have to do is to determine the size of the position.

For a 100,000 position (GBP/USD) the 20-pip move is equal to $200. Whether the amounts are negative or positive depend on whether you are short or long for every move.

You may take time to really study the P&L pip calculation, but this is not usually a concern since most online trading platforms will compute the P&L for you instantly, both realized when the trade is closed or unrealized if the trade is open.

However, calculating the P&L is crucial so you can effectively manage the risk and structure the trade. This will help you to understand the P&L implications of a trade strategy that you are considering so you can maintain your margin balance and gain control of your trade.

Really understanding your P&L can help you avoid costly mistakes such as placing a trade that is too high or placing stop loss orders beyond your price where your account falls under the needed margin. You need to at least compute the price point at which your position will be liquidated once your margin balance declines under the recommended ratio.

Interest Rates and Rollovers

One market norm that is peculiar to forex is rollover, which refers to a transaction where an open position from the settlement date is rolled over into the next value date.

The rollovers signify the intersection of interstate markets and forex. After all, currencies represent monetary value.

The rollover rates are based on the difference in interest rates of the two currency pairs that you are trading. This is because what you are actually trading is cash.

Yes, the currency is cash. When you go for long, it's similar to depositing cash into a bank. When you go for short, it's like you are borrowing money from a bank. Just as you would expect to earn interest from your bank deposits or pay interest for a loan, you should also expect an increase in holding a currency position over the changes in value.

The caveat in forex trading is that if you carry over an open position from value date to the next, the transaction involves two banks. One account has a positive balance (long) and the other account has a negative balance (short).

But because your accounts are in two different currencies, the two interest rates of the country using the currency will apply. *Interest rate differential* refers to the difference between the interest rates in the two countries. The bigger the interest-rate differential, the bigger the effect from rollovers. The lower the interest rate differential, the lesser the effect from rollovers. It is ideal to look for the benchmark or base lending rates for each country.

Leading financial market websites can provide you the relevant interest-rate levels. This includes www.fxstreet.com or www.marketwatch.com.

Bear in mind that rollover rates have a more significant impact on you, depending on the size of your position. They have a larger impact on someone trading in the millions compared to someone who is only trading in thousands.

But regardless of the size, it is still ideal to understand how a rollover can affect your trade. So it is important that you know how interest rates can affect the currency rates. After all, the interest rates are expressed in percentages and currency rates are in decimals.

Take note that the deposit rates can yield actual cash returns that are netted, and produce a net cash return. This net cash return is then dividend by the size position that provides the currency pips or the rollover rate.

Valuation Date and Trade Settlements

In discussing forex trading, we are implicitly referring to trading in the spot market, in which the securities are delivered immediately. In the real world, immediate means several business days. This allows banks and financial organizations to have time to settle a trade.

In forex trading, spot refers to the settlement of the trade in two business days, which is also known as the value date. The time is needed to allow for the processing of the trade across different time zones and for the currency payments to be completed around the globe.

Remember, the forex market operates on a 24-hour trade basis starting at 5 p.m. Eastern Time and ending the next day at 5 pm. So if today is Tuesday, spot currencies are trading for value on Thursday assuming there are no holidays in between.

On Tuesday 5 pm ET, the trade date becomes Wednesday and the value date is changed to Friday. If you have an open position on Tuesday at 5 pm ET closing, your position will be shifted to the next value date, in this case from Thursday to Friday or a rollover of one day.

If you completed the position the next day (Wednesday) and completed the trade date square, there are no rollovers because you don't have a position. The same is true if you

can't carry a position through the daily closing at 5 pm ET.

On Thursday trade dates, the spot currencies are usually trading for a Monday value date. On Wednesday 5 pm ET, the value date changes from Monday to Tuesday or known as a Weekend Rollover.

In this rollover computation, it will be a five-day rollover (Thursday, Friday, Saturday, Sunday, and Monday). Therefore, the cost of the rollover will be five times the usual daily cost. The only exception to the two-day spot convention in forex trading is USD/CAD because the primary financial centers in Canada and United States are sharing the same time zone. Therefore, wire transfers and communications can be easily processed.

It will only take one business day to settle USD/CAD trades. The weekend rollover for USD/CAD happens on Thursday after the 5 pm ET closing when the value date moves from Friday to Monday. This is only applicable to USD/CAD and not to other pairs that involve CAD such as EUR/CAD or CAD/JPY.

Value Dates and Market Holidays

Take note that value dates are based on individual currency pairs to consider banking holidays of countries involved. The rollovers can be longer when there's a banking holiday in one of the countries whose currency is part of the trade.

For instance, if it's Wednesday and you are trading CHF/USD, the typical value date would be Friday. However, if there's a banking holiday in Switzerland, Swiss banks are not open to settle the trade.

Therefore, the value date is adjusted to the next banking holiday that is common to Switzerland and the United States, usually the following Monday. In this case, the weekend rollover will take place at the closing of the trade on Tuesday at 5 pm ET when the value date would be shifted from Thursday to Monday (skipping over the holiday on Friday). This is a 4-day rollover.

What will happen at the change in value date at 5 pm ET (Wednesday)? There will be no rollover. Since the value date for trades made on Wednesday is already Monday, no rollover is required because the trades settled on Thursday are also for settlement on Monday. This is referred to as a double value date, which means two trade dates (Wednesday and Thursday) and are settling the same value date (Monday).

Several times every year (typically around Christmas, New Year, or Spring Break in Japan) when multiple banking holidays in different countries cross over several days, the rollover period could be as long as 7 or 8 days. Therefore, you may earn or pay seven or eight times the rollover fee in a single day, but you may not face any rollover fees for the remaining of the holiday period.

Rollover Transactions

Rollovers are typically performed by forex brokers if you hold an open position that has already passed the valuation date. Rollovers are applied to the open position by two offsetting trades, which result in the same open position. Some online forex brokers apply the rollover rates by changing the necessary rate for the open position.

Meanwhile, other forex brokers apply for the rollover credit or debit directly to the margin balance. Here are the important pointers you need to remember about rollovers:

- Forex brokers will apply rollovers to positions that are open after 5 pm ET

- Your broker will not apply rollovers if you are not carrying a position over the change in value date. Therefore, if you are square at the close of every trading session, then you don't need to worry about rollovers.

- Rollovers represent the cost of holding an open position or the interest rate return

- Rollovers represent the difference in interest rates between currency pairs in an open position. However, they are applied in currency-rate terms

- Rollovers are composed of net interest you have paid or you have earned, depending on the movement of your position

- You can earn money through rollovers if you get short a currency with the lower interest rate and go long a currency with a higher interest rate

- You will lose money if you long a currency with the lower interest rates and short a currency with the higher interest rate

- Some forex brokers apply spreads to rollovers that can deduct any interest earned by your position

- Rollover credits/costs are based on the size of your position - the bigger the position, the bigger the gain or cost to you

- You should consider rollovers as a business expense and should not be considered as a catalyst in your trading decisions

If you will trade a relatively big account with an online forex broker (around $25,000) it is possible to negotiate a tighter rollover spread. This will allow you to capture more of the profits if you are in the right position or you can reduce the cost.

Currency Prices 101

We will now begin exploring how actual forex trading works. But before that, it is first important to get a glimpse of the mechanism behind currency prices. If you want to become a forex day trader, you should always be mindful of currency prices.

When you are trading in the forex market, you are trading a currency pair. And when you buy something, you should be always mindful of the price. So in this section, we'll take a look at how online forex brokers show currency prices so you can properly execute a trade.

Different brokers use different formats to present currency prices in their platforms. A comprehensive picture of what the currency prices mean will allow you to navigate the various platforms used by forex brokers and also help you identify important features that can help you in the trade.

Bids and Offers

Whenever you use a forex trading terminal, you will typically see two prices for each currency pair.

The number on the left is referred to as the bid and the number on the right is referred to as the offer or the ask. Some brokers present the numbers on top (offer) and bottom (bid). An easy way to tell the difference between the numbers is that the bid price is always lower compared to the offer.

Currency price quotes have two parts - the deal price and the big price. The latter refers to the first 3 numbers of the entire currency rate and is usually show in a faded font or smaller font.

On the other hand, the deal price refers to the last two digits of the currency pair and is usually shown in a brighter font or a larger font.

Spread

This refers to the difference between the bid and offer prices. Many online forex brokers are using spread as the basis of their platforms, especially for retail forex traders.

Basically, the spread serves as the charges or the commission that your brokers will charge you for facilitating the trade. While some brokers promote their service as "zero commission" chances are they are still earning from the spread.

The spread is also regarded as the remuneration that forex brokers receive from being an important player in the market. It varies from one broker to another and will also depend on the currency pair that you are trading.

The spread is generally lower if the currency pair is more liquid. Bigger spreads could result in less liquid currency pair. This is especially true for cross currencies.

Trade Execution

In the Final Chapter, we will explore the steps in signing up for your own forex account. Ideally, you should first register with a demo account so you can get a feel for executing deals before you spend your own money for forex trading.

There are two main ways to execute a forex trade - live trading and orders through a broker.

In live trading, you can access the market platforms to trade currency pairs at current prices. Remember, you should have a solid trading plan before you execute a trade because once you make a live deal, it is already settled.

What about if you suddenly changed your mind during a live trade? You have to execute another trade so you can correct the mistake. This is usually expensive as changing minds in the market will cost you money.

There are different ways to enter the forex market, and this will all depend on the setup of your preferred broker. Most brokers have live-streaming functions that will allow you to quickly see the prices and enter into the deal with only several clicks.

Many online brokers now also have their own mobile apps that you can easily use for quick forex trading. Only a few years ago, day traders had to use devices that must be plugged into a desktop computer or a specialized terminal.

With the introduction of forex trading apps, retail traders can now participate in the market using their phones anytime and anywhere. Today, you can trade while watching your kid play basketball or waiting for your order to arrive in a restaurant.

But mobile phone trading also has its disadvantages. For instance, if your smartphone has unreliable internet connection or your battery is low, then there's the risk of going offline when you are executing a trade.

Below are helpful tips when you are trading on your mobile phone:

- Before you execute a trade, make sure that your battery is enough to sustain online trading.

- Avoid trading if you are currently in a place with bad mobile reception. You may lose money if you can't monitor your trade.

- Maximize your internet connection by closing other apps while you are trading.

Orders

Orders are generally used by forex day traders to take advantage of profitable market movements even if they are not able to execute a trade personally. Remember, the forex market never closes so a considerable movement may happen while you are sleeping.

Many forex traders have their other occupations that also require focus. In order to respond to the market without being there, you can use orders. Day traders use orders in order to:

- Protect profits and minimize losses
- Capture sharp price fluctuations
- Minimize risk in highly volatile windows
- Automatically execute a trade from entry to exit
- Safeguard trading capital from significant losses

The forex market can be extremely volatile and usually difficult to predict. With orders, you can capitalize on short-term market movements and also place a limit on any adverse effect of price movements.

Effective use of orders can also help you in quantifying the risk that you are taking. A sound forex trading strategy should always include a solid strategy for using orders.

Types of Orders

Bear in mind that not all types of orders are available for day traders. So you should always ask your broker about the orders you can use before you sign up with any account.

Stop Loss Orders

Forex traders use this type of order to limit the possible losses when the market is moving against your current position. Without a stop loss order in place, you are exposing your trade to a high risk.

If you are in a short position, then the order for stop loss is to buy at a higher price compared to the prevailing rate in the market.

If you are in a long position, then the order for stop loss is to sell at a lower price compared to the prevailing rate in the market.

Trailing Stop Loss Orders

Seasoned forex day traders know how to quickly stop losing positions and allow their winning trades to take profit as much as they can.

You can mimic this strategy through a trailing stop loss order. When you have a winning trade, you can wait for the next market to follow a reversal and take you out instead of choosing the right exit. A trailing stop loss order will allow you to work on a fixed number of pips from your entry rate.

NOTE: Not all brokers can provide you with a trailing stop loss order. If the platform you have chosen doesn't have this feature, you can copy the trailing stop but you have to do it manually by changing the rate on your usual stop loss order. But this is still dragging especially if you are not a full time day trader.

Take Profit Orders

This type of order is used by forex traders to automatically close a trade if the position reaches a specific predetermined level.

For example, if you buy a currency pair CAD/USD at 1.1780 and you add a take profit order at 1.800, the trade will be closed and the profit will be protected if the currency pair reaches the 1.800 level.

This order is automatic so you don't need to constantly keep track of the market for the best time to exit.

If you set a take profit order, you also need to set up an order for stop loss. This move is quite similar to a take profit order but this one is designed to minimize your possible losses when the market doesn't follow a lucrative trend.

Take profit order is an important tool for retail traders because it safeguards your profits when there's a sharp reversal in the market. Remember, the forex market is highly volatile and the trades can easily change from making money to losing money in a matter of minutes.

This order is usually used by traders who use fundamental metrics such as the average true range that can help in determining the best way to enter or exit points.

Also take note that take profit orders are commonly established based on your trading plan. This order can be opened short or long depending on your position.

Ideally, you should set this order at a higher level if your trading plan is based on a significant movement in the market. On the other hand, you should place a closer take profit if your fundamental strategy is to protect your profit before any market turn.

It is usually a false assumption that taking profit in the short-term will allow you to sustain a positive capital and beat the market. This rarely happens. Some traders take profit levels too close to the opening price, which usually leads to losses.

As a newbie trader, it is essential for you to understand the basic principles of financial management to make certain that you will actually win the game.

In figuring out where to place your take profit order, resistance and support levels are also crucial. When to take profit and market direction can help you determine market lows and highs. A fundamental viewpoint in this case is to take profit before high-impact price movements.

Remember to focus on major price levels and just ignore the horizontal lines in a forex chart.

Limit Orders

Some newbie forex traders are confused over take profit and limit orders. This is not surprising because a take profit order is actually a form of a limit order.

The primary difference is that take-profit orders will minimize or close open positions. Meanwhile, limit orders open new positions or add to prevailing positions in the same line of movement.

Take note that limit order pertains to any order that activates a favorable trade compared to the prevailing market price. At this point, you should always remember the classic mantra in trading - buy low and sell high.

If you place a limit order to buy, then the trade execution is entered at a price under the current market price. If you place a limit order to sell, then the trade execution is entered into a price that is better than the current market price.

OCO Order

OCO is abbreviation for One-Cancels-The-Other Order. This is a special type of a stop loss order, which is usually added with a take profit order. It serves as a stand-by protection order for open positions.

In this order, your forex position shall stay open until one of your existing order levels is triggered by the market. The effect is closing the position. If your position reaches an order level and triggered, the other order will be quickly cancelled.

Contingent Orders

You may also choose to combine several forms of orders in building a solid strategy for your trade. You may use contingent orders to place on your trade even if you can't go online. This usually provides peace of mind to traders knowing that your contingent order has all the bases covered and you are clear in your defined risks.

Contingent orders are also known as if-then orders because it requires the IF order to be fulfilled first before the second part to be triggered.

Chapter 5 – Making Sense of Forex Market News

"Don't blindly follow someone, follow market and try to hear what it is telling you." -
Jaymin Shah

At any given moment, any number of real-world forces are at work in the forex market. This includes geopolitical events, interest rate decisions, and economic data.

These forces are filtered through the collective consciousness of the market and translated into price actions. As a forex trader, you need to focus on trying to make profits based on the price movements. But bear in mind that you are not the only trader in the market.

Hundreds of thousands are also active in the forex market, and they are all assessing the same information and data, but more likely they are working on different assumptions.

To provide another perspective, the trades are based on different conclusions that is what ultimately moves currency prices. This will bring you back to the observation - if it's not one thing it's another. This all boils down on how the forex markets process information and there are a lot of information out there.

Even seasoned traders who think they have seen it all can still be mesmerized by new and unexpected outcomes in the market. Hence, you are not alone when it comes to making sense of market information just to make immediate trading decisions.

Your objective is to avoid "paralysis by analysis" and to absorb and understand as much as you can about the market drivers. The goal is to make successful forex traders. Hopefully, this book will provide you a better understanding of the types of market information that drives the market so you can effectively interpret and apply this information.

Where to Source Market Information

Before you can analyze tons of information about the market, you first need to know where to source information in the first place. Organizational traders employ teams of strategists, analysts, and economists to provide them with real-time observations and interpretations.

But don't worry as any information that these big traders are getting are also available to retail traders. However, you should exert extra effort to find, read, and make sense of it.

Have you ever boarded a moving car?

The art of boarding a moving car requires you to begin running alongside the running car before you grab a handle and board. If you are just there flat-footed and you try to board, you will lose your arm.

This is an ideal metaphor to describe the forex market.

Any day trader who will try to jump in without first getting up to speed will be up for failure. Getting up to speed in the forex market means learning what present themes are driving the market. In order to do this, you need to know where to find market sources and how to interpret information.

However, getting up to speed will take some time. Therefore, you should not be in a rush to begin trading based on several hours or days of reading. Ideally, you should dedicate a month worth of research on different currency pairs. You should also familiarize yourself with what is going on before you consider yourself ready to board a moving train.

One way to prepare yourself for the forex market is to use a demo account offered by online forex broker. In just a month, you will experience a full cycle of economic data indicators as well as majority of market events such as central bank meetings that will provide you a first-hand experience of how the market moves and shifts to new market information.

An exciting part of forex trading is that there's always something going on. Remember, a busy road is filled with running cars. So don't worry about missing your ride because there's always another one that will come for you.

Market Pulse

With the popularity of online forex trading in recent years, there's been a growth of currency-specific online sources that are catering to the needs of day traders.

To save space, we will not review these sites in this book, but you should check out www.fxstreet.com, which is a site that features different sources of forex market analysis.

Twitter is also another reliable source of information, particularly around important news releases and breaking news events. If you're looking at forex research from different information sources, you need to be mindful of who has provided the analysis.

If you are not aware of the backgrounds or identities of the forex analysts, you might be relying on the work of someone who just have few months of market experience. This is not exactly a sophisticated insight.

If you are in doubt, you should focus on the reports that are developed by market analysts you really trust or major financial organizations. Many online forex trading platforms also provide different types of market research and analysis, so if you're deciding which broker you must open your account with, you should look at the quality of its research.

Sources of News

In the past, people tend to focus on mainstream financial press that provide continuous coverage of the major financial markets including forex.

Their websites offer regular intraday updates that can cover data releases and announcements, typically with some organizational commentary, too. This will allow you to better understand the reasons behind market behavior. The best sources of financial news are Reuters, MarketWatch, and Bloomberg.

Some of the most credible analysts tweet their insights throughout the day, and you can also follow most of the major news outlets to gain a fast perspective of what is happening.

There are also reliable blogs such as Baby Pips and Forex Factory. Be sure to check out several sources and narrow down to the ones that are working for you. Just keep in mind that what you will read from these sources has already happened, and the market has digested the information and so the prices might have been adjusted accordingly.

In interpreting news and information, you should always ask yourself the source of the information as you must always differentiate fact from rumor or opinion.

Moreover, you should also try to figure out how old the information is. You have to gauge the timeliness of the news and the extent to which the market has already responded on it.

Sources for Real-Time Market Information

The forex market moves on information quite fast, and the organizational players basically have different live feeds from the primary accredited news sources such as Reuters, Bloomberg, and Dow Jones.

Nowadays, one of the fastest ways to obtain real-time news, particularly information releases is from Twitter that provides you access to unlimited news sourced and could be an effective way to access real-time market news.

Event Calendars and Economic Data

The forex market revolves around economic events and data, and you need to find a reliable market calendar so you can see what is coming down the road next.

Ideally, you should look for market calendars that contain all the major upcoming economic releases showing the time of the update, the market forecast, and the previous report cited.

Aside from data reports, you should also keep an eye on economic events such as central bank rate-setting meetings, the issuance of the minutes of those meetings, speeches by chief bankers, and significant meetings such as monthly gatherings of finance ministers.

Insights from these events usually move the market in the short term and if you are not watchful of them, you could be blindsided. In a bit, we will discuss how the forex market anticipates events and information, and how this behavior can affect the prices. But at this point, you should understand that you can't anticipate anything that you don't know.

Currency Forecasts

Many of the financial media are keen on organizational predictions of where the forex market is headed, and you will likely encounter a lot of monthly, quarterly, and yearly exchange rate forecasts in your market research.

However, you should treat these as indicators of general market sentiment and outlook rather than solid trading advice. Many forecasts are heavily skewed to present circumstances and are a much better guide to what the market is really thinking at the moment compared to where rates will actually be in the next few months.

Gossip

Despite its professional image, the financial markets are also susceptible to gossip. True or untrue, rumors may still affect the market behavior in the forex world.

One example of gossip that drives the market is called the whisper numbers, which are rumors of economic data prior to its scheduled release. These rumors have the tendency to roil short-term market positions that traders opened in anticipation of an economic report, and they also affect the subsequent reaction of the market to the report.

For instance, a whisper number that suggests a bad picture of a data report from the US, which was originally predicted to be weak in the first place, may see the USD come under extreme pressure before the release date.

If the real number is revealed and it's weak but still in line with the forecasts, but not as low as projected by the whisper number, then the USD could rebound because the worst fears were not true.

On the other hand, large market orders are rumors that usually hold water, but not certain or absolute. These are normally linked with large organizational players or central banks that are trading in the forex market.

The typically mention a price level, so pay attention to the price level as a possible source of resistance or support. When the price level is broken, the order either wasn't real or has already been filled. In both cases, the price level has given way, possibly triggering a further directional move.

Nowadays, gossips spread fast, and day traders usually have to contend with them several times every day, which in due time may reduce the effects on the market.

The problem with gossip is that there's no easy way to figure out if they are true and even if you can, you have no way to be sure of the price reaction that is ultimately the key to deal with gossip.

Surprisingly, gossips have the uncanny habit of spreading after relatively extensive attempts to break through significant technical levels or directions moves.

You should take note that a technical level test or intraday move is underway. A tight strategy for exit is also crucial to protect your trades if that market turns tail. If there's unproven information behind a sudden reversal, you can typically find out only after the fact anyway. However, a tight exit plan could save you from getting left behind in the reversals.

Market Themes

At any given point in the forex market, several themes can dominate the attention of the market. Market themes are at the core of actual forces presently affecting the market. These are what market analysts and commentators are talking about when they are trying to explain what is happening in the market.

But on top of that, themes serve as the filters through which new data and information are digested by the market. They all come in different sizes and shapes and they have different effects on the market over time.

Some are longer themes that can activate the direction of the market for months or even years, such as the persistence of the US trade deficit. Other themes may only hold for weeks, days or even a few hours such as a controversial tweet from a central banker.

Market themes generally come in two primary forms that are co-existing in parallel universes but they also overlap a lot of times. The two main forms of themes that we like to focus on are technical themes and fundamental themes that we will discuss in the later chapters.

Currency Fundamental Drivers

Every currency has its own set of fundamental factors in which it is being assessed by the market.

The basic fundamental environment is all present, but it is also subject to change similar to economic conditions that will change in the course of business cycles.

Fundamental themes will also change in relative importance to one another, with specific themes being pushed to the side for a specific period if events or news focus the attention of the market on other, more important themes.

As you continue, bear in mind that each theme is applicable to each and every currency but in different degrees at any given moment. You will learn some examples of what will probably happen to a currency based on the context of information means for each theme.

Interest Rates Movement

Interest rates are typically the single most important factor that drives the value of a currency. However, it's

not just about where the interest rate levels are now, even though this is still undeniably important.

What really matters most is the general direction, their level in the future, and the timing of any changes. Remember, financial markets are always speculating on the direction of interest rates, although the interest rate changes are relatively not frequent.

For instance, as of press time, the Bank of England hasn't changed the interest rates level since 2009. The

interest rate changes and speculation over the market direction are the primary drivers of the value of a currency on a daily basis as well as over longer time frames.

The data inputs that drive the interest rate outlook are focused on inflation reports and economic growth data. Take note that the stronger the growth picture, the higher the inflation pressures are. This will result in interest rates to move higher, typically improving the outlook of a currency.

If the inflation readings are lower or the growth outlook is weaker, the interest rates are more likely to move lower or remain steady, usually damaging the currency in the long run.

Bond markets also have a huge impact on the direction of interest rates and are considered the best real-time measurement tool for interest rate markets. The central banks can only affect short-term interest rates that are driven by the target interest rate of the central bank.

However, longer-term bond yields with the 10-year maturity as measurement tools can reflect the long-term view of the market as well as the direction of future interest rate movements.

Lower interest rates in bonds could point to a weaker economic perspective and the possibility of lower interest rates ahead. This can usually damage the currency while higher yields could result in a positive economic outlook and the possibility of higher rates, normally supporting the currency.

The influence of interest rate themes can be felt by the market if the interest rates of the two currencies are seen to diverge - when one interest rate of a currency is expected to move higher and the other is lower or at the same level.

For relative changes that may favor one currency over the other, you should keep track of the three-month yield spreads - the difference between the yields of two government bonds. However, rates don't necessarily

have to diverge to affect currencies. The yield of one currency may just move higher faster than another, and the widening spread between the two will be apparent in the long run.

Growth Prospects

Economic growth outlook is the linchpin to several factors that determine the value of a currency. This includes the attractiveness of a nation's investment climate, and the interest rate outlook.

Not surprisingly, the stronger the growth prospect, the better a specific currency is likely to perform relative to currencies of countries with weaker growth prospects.

Stronger growth of the economy can increase the probability of higher interest rates down the road as central banks usually seek to limit rapid growth to head off inflationary strain.

Meanwhile, weaker growth data increases the prospect of potentially lower interest rates as well as damaging the outlook for investment. Numerous data reports for growth reflect only a specific sector of a country's bigger economy such as the real estate market or the manufacturing industry.

Depending on how important that sector is to the bigger national economy, those reports have the tendency to be interpreted as more or less important.

For example, industrial production is more important in Japan compared to the US because of the more significant role manufacturing plays in Japan. Also, there's no fix recipe for how growth data will affect the value of a currency, but if the interest rate outlook is basically neutral, as in no solid conviction on the movement of the rates of the two currencies, the growth theme becomes more significant.

Combating Inflation

As a forex trader, you need to monitor fiscal policy developments. The inflation theme has more nuances compared to the growth theme in terms of its implications to the value of a currency.

Depending on the bigger picture, it may produce starkly different result for a currency. Basically, if there is a good outlook for growth, and inflation is too high, you can say that it is a forex plus.

On the other hand, if the growth is weakening or low, and inflation is too high, you can say that it is forex negative. In both cases, the interest rates could be steady to high. However, a low-slow growth case added with high/higher interest rates increases the risks of an economy falling into a recession that could ultimately lead to interest rate cuts.

In view of this, currencies are a bit fickle in that they are attracted to higher interest rates some of the time, but not always. The same scenario happens if a central bank is holding rates that are too high for too long, normally based on combating inflation, and the market starts to speculate that an economic hardship is imminent.

This market behavior is actually not unusual if you think that the forex market is basically always looking for future interest rates. In considering inflation data into the interest rate theme, you should be aware of how the general growth theme is holding up. If there's

good growth, and inflation is high due to economic strength, higher inflation readings will be supportive of the currency.

If there's a slowdown and inflation is still high, the impact on the currency will be less positive and probably downright negative.

Financial Stability

The Eurozone Debt Crisis (2009 to 2013) and the Great Financial Crisis in the US (2008 to 2009) shone light to financial stability as another general theme in the forex market.

During the early days of the crisis, the financial players (banks and insurance companies) was deeply affected and needed massive intervention from the government to avoid a meltdown.

The succeeding economic turmoil later revealed excessive government debt levels as well as budget deficits as a threat to economic growth and sovereign debt.

The journey to recovery among developed countries remain a difficult choice and the levels of government debt and the risk for sovereign default still looms.

Regardless if it is quantitative easing in the United States or high debt levels in Europe, financial stability and perceptions of credit ratings can sway over national currencies, typically for the worse.

One way to measure market fears is to keep track of government bond yields. Higher bond yields could mean investors are selling bonds over fears of a default and not because of growth expectations. Therefore, the currency at risk may suffer alongside government bonds.

Measuring the Strength of Structural Themes

Beyond financial stability, inflation, growth, and interest rates, several other significant themes usually assert themselves, mostly in the structural aspect or the general picture of how the economy is performing.

Bear in mind that structural themes can be fleeting. They may be in full force today but can drop altogether tomorrow. These themes are normally peripheral to those we have discussed in the previous sections, but they can still exert important influence on currency pairs by their own right.

In addition, they can also boost the impact of the main themes similar to throwing kerosene to a fire. Here are the basic recurring structural themes:

- **Deficits** - Both trade and fiscal deficits are normally considered as forex negatives. During times of low to slow growth, the effect of deficits can be magnifies as the credibility of a currency is scrutinized such as the case with euro. In times of stable or high growth, deficits could have less influence but are still a negative hanging over the general prospect.

- **Employment** - Employment is an important factor in the long-term performance of an economy and the main driver of interest rates. As long as employment is increasing, the long-term economic outlook will be supported. However, if the employment growth starts to falter, as reflected in the labor reports, the economic outlook will tend to be marked down. Sharp unemployment increases are among the triggers to interest rate cuts by central banks, which goes back to the main interest rate theme.

- **Geopolitics** - Political tensions were not always all-present as they seem today, from trade war against China, to North Korean nuclear tests, to upheaval in the Middle East. During times of geopolitical tension, safe currencies such as Swiss franc and Japanese yen tend to outperform the riskier currencies such as NZD or AUD. Considering the size of the American economy and wide military involvement, the USD is also vulnerable. When geopolitical tensions subside, the market is fast to revert to pre-existing conditions.

- **Government changes or uncertainty** - Government changes and uncertainty in the political climate can certainly damage the sentiment of the market towards the concerned currency. But immediately after the issues are resolved, political issues tend to quickly fade.

Technical Themes Assessment

Technical themes are probably a bit harder to understand compared to fundamental themes especially if you are not familiar with technical analysis.

But to put this more simply, there are instances that currency prices move simply because currency prices are moving. The fundamental political or economic themes may not have dramatically changed, but the price levels have, and this is usually enough to bring primary market interest out of the guesswork.

In many cases, breaks of major price or technical levels will be in the direction suggested by the prevailing fundamental themes, but the timing is usually suspect and could leave traders dubious. However, sizeable price movements tend to take a life on their own, forcing market players to take action based on price shifts alone.

Moreover, the prevalence of technical analysis as the fundamentals for numerous trading decisions could add weight to current fundamental-driven activities, generating yet another theme to drive the movement. This is the technical theme.

It could be a trending market movement, which attracts trend-following forex traders who don't care about the

underlying fundamentals. These traders will keep on pushing the market in the direction it is going, possibly beyond what the fundamentals would dictate.

If a currency pair has broken through significant technical levels, it can attract breakout traders - speculator who focus on jumping on breaks of key price levels, searching to participate on the move for an easy trade. However, nothing will be easy, and breakout forex traders may take the hit if the breaks are not true and the ranges will survive.

The added interest entering the market in the direction of the market again propels price faster than it may regularly go. Getting a sense of where a currency pair stands from a technical perspective is always crucial even if you don't base the trades on technical analysis. The technical theme also stems from different actual considerations that all relate back to the currency prices.

Options Interest

The forex options market is huge and considered as one of the reasons that the spot market is as massive as it is. Options hedging is one of the largest sources of spot market movement outside short-term spot speculation. If spot prices have been trading in popular regions, option interest has the tendency to accrue caused by any considerable changes in the market.

When the ranges are broken, sizeable option-related interest is often pushed to emerge into the market and leverage the movement of the price breakout. This could sustain new exposures or unwind your financial hedges.

Hedgers

Hedgers are forced to participate in the market when a rapid and unexpected price movement develops. Different firms identify an inner hedging rate for corporate and financial management purposes. As long as they are capable of selling above or buying below the rate, they are looking good. When the market moves sharply, they could be forced to jump in on the direction for fear of not ever seeing the inner hedging rate again.

Consensus Expectations

Take note that data reports and news events don't just happen right away. The forex markets evaluate incoming data reports that are relative to market forecasts, normally referred to as consensus expectations or just consensus.

Consensus expectations refer to the average economic forecasts made by economists from leading financial organizations, academe, or private investments firms. News agencies such as Reuters and Bloomberg ask economists for their projections of upcoming information collate the results.

The outcome average forecast is what appears on market calendars, which indicate what is expected for any given data report. The consensus will then become the baseline against which the incoming data will be assessed by the market.

For economic data, the market will compare the actual result - the economic figure, which is actually reported against the consensus (what was expected). The actual data is usually interpreted by the market in the following ways:

- Worse Than Expected - The data is weaker than the projected consensus. For reports on inflation, a worse-than-projected reading could signify that the inflation was higher than forecast, or more inflationary.

- In Line or As Expected - The actual data report was at or quite close to the consensus prediction.

- Better Than Expected - The report was basically stronger than the consensus prediction. A better-than-projected reading on inflation reports means inflation is lower than expected or more benign.

- As Expected or In Line With Expectations - The actual data report was at or very near the projected consensus.

Moreover, the degree to which a data report is better or worse than predicted is crucial. The deviation to the report will affect the release of the data. In assessing central bank statements and commentary from monetary policy makers, the market is assessing the language used in terms of leaning towards steady to lower interest rates (dovish) or leaning towards increasing interest rates (hawkish).

Chapter 6 – Forex Theories and Models

"The goal of a successful trader is to make the best trades. Money is secondary." - Alexander Elder

There are several theories and models behind the foreign exchange market. While you don't have to master them all, it is still ideal to understand the general ideas behind the research.

The primary economic theories found in the forex market are more about the parity settings. Basically, parity refers to the economic justification of the price at which the currency pairs must be traded according to important factors such as interest rates and inflation. According to these economic theories, if the parity setting cannot sustain, there is an arbitrage opportunity for market players.

But arbitrage opportunities, like in other markets are often immediately discovered and discarded before even providing the individual investor the chance for capitalization. Other forex market theories are based on economic factors such as capital flows, trade, and how the country is running its monetary operations.

Asset Market Model

In the Asset Market Model, you have to look into the flow of money into a country from foreign sources for buying assets such as bonds, stocks, and other financial assets.

If you see that the country is experiencing large surge of foreign investments, the price of its currency will rise as the domestic currency has to be purchased by these foreign investments. This model also considers the capital account of the balance in comparison to the present account.

This model is popular among forex investors as the capital accounts of countries are beginning to significantly surpass the current account as foreign money flow increases.

Balance of Payments Theory

There are two divisions in a country's balance of payments -

the capital account and the current account. These two measure the outflows and inflows of goods and capital of a country.

In the balance of payments theory, you have to look at the present account that deals with tangible goods trade so you can get a general direction of the exchange rate.

One indicator that a country's exchange rate is not in balance is if it runs a large current account deficit and surplus. In order to adjust to this condition, the exchange rate should be adjusted gradually.

Look if the country is running more deficit (higher imports vs exports) as the currency is more likely to depreciate. Meanwhile, a surplus (higher export versus import) will lead to the appreciation of the country's currency.

You can determine the balance of payments of a country by using the formula below:

BCA + BKA + BRA =

BCA refers to the present account balance

BKA refers to the capital account balance

BRA refers to the reserves account balance

Economic Data

Economic theories could affect the movement of the currencies in the long-run. When it comes to daily or weekly transactions, forex players focus more on economic data.

Countries are often regarded as the largest companies in the world and that holding currency is basically getting a share of that country. Economic data like the current Gross Domestic

Product (GDP) figures are usually regarded to be similar to the latest earnings data of a company.

In a similar manner that current events and financial news could influence the stock price of a company, news involving a country could also have a significant effect on the movement of the currency of that country.

Significant changes in the political condition, GDP, consumer confidence, unemployment rate, inflation, and interest rates could result in substantial losses or gains depending on the nature of the news and the present situation of the country.

The volume of economic news that you might need to monitor every day from around the world could be overwhelming. However, as you go along the forex market, it will become a lot more clear which news could have the largest influence. Below are several economic factors that are basically regarded to have the biggest influence in the foreign exchange market.

Retail Sales

The data on retail sales measures the volume of sales that retailers have gained during the period. This basically reflects spending in the country. The data does not cover all stores, but only monitors a basket of stores of different types to gain an idea on how people are spending.

This data will provide you a general ideal of the country's economic stability. In general, strong spending indicates a strong economy. In the United States, the retail sales data is released by the Department of Commerce once a year.

Employment Data

Another economic indicator that you should take a look when you are into forex is the employment data or the number of people who are currently employed in the country.

In the United States, this data is called non-farm payrolls and published by the Bureau of Labor Statistics every first Friday of the month. In most instances, strong increase in employment shows that a country is experiencing a strong economy, while the opposite means otherwise.

If a particular country is going through significant problems in the economy, strong employment data could affect the currency price, because it is an indicator that the economy is recovering.

Meanwhile, high employment could result to inflation, so this indicator might affect the currency price. To put it simply, the movement of currency and economic data will usually depend on the circumstances that are prevailing if the data is released.

Gross Domestic Product (GDP)

The GDP of a country is used as a measurement of all the completed goods and services that a country has produced during a specific period of time. Calculating the GDP is divided into four divisions: total net exports, business spending, government spending, and private consumption.

Economists regard GDP as the best measurement of the economic health of a country with GDP increases indicating economic growth. As you already know, a healthy economy entices more foreign investments.

This will usually lead to increases in the currency value, as the money moves into the country. In the United States, this information is published by the Bureau of Economic Analysis.

Durable Goods

Durable goods refers to those who can last longer than three years such as automobiles, gadgets, and home appliances. The data for durable goods is used to measure the volume of manufactured goods that are produced and shipped for a particular period of time.

This data will provide you a general idea of the amount of individual expenditure on these goods on top of the information on the health of a specific sector. In the United States, this data is published by the Department of Commerce.

Capital and Trade Flows

Transactions between countries build large cash flows, which could have a significant effect on the currency value. Remember, a country that is importing more than its exports may experience depreciation on its currency because of its need to bid its own money to buy the exporting nation's currency. Moreover, higher investments in a country could lead to significant increases in the currency value.

The data on trade flow takes a closer look at the difference between the exports and imports of a country. There is a trade deficit if the imports are higher than exports.

In the United States, the Department of Commerce publishes the trade flow data every month. This shows the volume of goods and services that the country has imported and exported during the previous month.

Meanwhile, the data on capital flow focuses on the fine distinction in the currency volume that is surging through exports or investments to currency that is being offered for foreign imports or investments.

In general, there will be a surplus of capital flow if a country is enjoying a high volume of foreign investments where foreign investors are buying domestic assets like real estate and stocks.

The combined total of the trade and capital flow of a country is known as balance of payments data. This is divided into three categories: financial account, the capital account, and current account.

The financial account focuses on the cash flow between countries mainly for investments. The capital account focuses on the exchange of cash between countries for the purpose of buying capital assets. The current account focuses on the flow of goods and services between countries.

Macroeconomic and Geopolitical Events

The most extreme fluctuations in the foreign exchange market is often influenced by geopolitical and macroeconomic events such as financial crises, changes in the monetary policy, elections, and wars. These can all change or reshape the economic condition of the country, which includes its market fundamentals.

For instance, an election gridlock in a country could place a large strain on the economy of a country and may affect the volatility in the region and thus affecting the currency value. In forex trading, it is important that you are updated on these geopolitical and macroeconomic events.

Interest Rate Parity (IRP)

IRP is quite similar to PPP, because it suggests that there should be no arbitrage opportunities if the two assets in two countries have the same interest rates and the risks for each country is also virtually the same.

The law of one price is also the basis of IRP, because purchasing one asset in one country must also yield the same return as the same asset in another country. Otherwise, the exchange rates will have to be adjusted to bridge the difference.

Below is the formula for getting the IRP:

$$(i_1 - i_2) = (\frac{F - S}{S})(1 - i_2)$$

F - refers to the exchange rate in the forwards market

S - refers to the exchange rate in the spot market

I_1 - refers to the interest rate in country 1

I_2 - refers to the exchange rate in country 2

In terms of interest rates, the most concentration by market participants is placed more on the bank rate changes of the country's central bank. This is used for monetary

adjustment and establishment of the monetary policy of the country.

In the United States, the bank rate is determined by the Federal Open Market Committee (FOMC). This rate is used by commercial banks for lending and borrowing to the US Treasury.

The FOMC convenes eight times every year to discuss the current economic factors and decide whether to lower, raise, or not change the bank rate. Forex market participants should take note of the outcome of these meetings to guide you in forex trading.

Monetary Model

This forex model concentrates on the monetary policy of a country to help in figuring out the exchange rate.

The monetary policy of a country primarily deals with the supply of money in the country, which is determined by the amount of money printed by the treasury as well as the interest rate set by the central bank.

Countries that adopt a monetary policy, which quickly grows its supply will likely experience inflationary pressure because of the increased circulation. This may lead to currency devaluation.

Purchasing Power Parity (PPP)

PPP is an economic theory, which states that the price levels between two countries must be equivalent to each other after adjustments in the exchange rate. This theory is founded on the one price law, in which the cost of a similar good must be the same regardless of the location.

According to this theory, if there is one major difference between two countries for the same product after the adjustment in the exchange rate, there is a need to create an arbitrage since the product could be obtained from the country, which can sell it for a cheaper price.

Below is PPP's relative version:

$$e = \frac{\pi_1 - \pi_2}{1 + \pi_2}$$

e - refers to the change rate in the exchange rate

'π_1 - refers to the rate of inflation in country 1

'π_2 - refers to the rate of inflation in country 2

For instance, let's say that the inflation rate of country A is 10% and the rate of inflation in country B is 5%, then country A's currency must appreciate at least 4.76% against that of country B.

Real Interest Rate Differentiation Model

This forex theory basically suggests that countries with higher real interest rates will likely experience an increase in their currencies compared to countries with lower interest rates.

The main reason behind this is that investors are more likely to invest their money in countries with higher real estate interest rates so they can earn higher returns. The country with the higher real estate interest rate will likely bid up its currency exchange rate.

Theory and Practice in the Forex Market

Understanding these foreign exchange theories could help you understand the underlying principles of the forex market and how it affects or affected by economy.

But take note that there are theories that are conflict with each other, so there is no certainty that these are not 100% accurate to help you in projecting the fluctuations in the forex market. Their application may likely vary according to the market conditions, but it is still crucial to know the core concepts behind these theories.

At this point, you might be a bit overwhelmed by the large volume of data that is being published and that you should monitor as you try forex trading. In spite of this, it is crucial to know what news announcements could affect the currencies that you are betting your money on.

After understanding the economic factors that are driving the foreign exchange market, we will next take a look at the two primary strategies that you can use in trading in the forex market - fundamental analysis and technical analysis.

Chapter 7 - Fundamental Analysis and Fundamental Strategies in Forex Trading

"I believe in analysis and not forecasting." - Nicolas Darvas

In the stock market, fundamental analysis measures the true value of a company. A fundamentalist (one who mainly use fundamental analysis) base his decision to invest or trade in stocks according to the calculation.

Somehow, this is similar in the foreign exchange market, where fundamentalists are also looking into the true value of the countries and their currencies. They are also watching out for economic announcements in order to gain an idea of the true value of the currency.

In general, geo-political events, economic data, and news reports from a certain country are regarded similarly to announcements about stocks and companies used by investors to gain insight of their true value. The value may change over time because of several factors including financial strength and growth. Fundamentalists are focusing on this data to assess the currency of the countries in the currency pair that he is interested in.

In this Chapter, we will discuss the top forex fundamental strategies that are used by traders and investors today.

Forex Investment Strategy - Forex Carry Trade

The forex carry trade is an investment strategy wherein a trader is offering a currency that has lower interest rates and buys a currency with higher interest rate. To put it simply, you are lending currencies at a higher rate and borrow at a lower rate. In using this strategy, you can make profits through the difference between these two rates.

Remember, when you are leveraging a trade, even a slight movement between the rates could result to great profits or greater losses. Aside from capturing the differences on the rates, the traders also focuses on the increasing value of the currency, because money flows into the currency that is high-yielding that increases its value,

One good example of this is the carry trade of the Japanese yen in 1999, when the country lowered its interest rates to almost 0%. Investors eventually capitalized on these lower interest rates by borrowing substantial amount of Japanese yen, which was converted into USD to purchase US treasury bonds.

These bonds guaranteed as high as 5%. Because the Japanese interest rate was basically zero, the investors are not paying any substantial amount to borrow yen and made a lot of profit from the US treasury bonds. Through proper leverage, you can substantially increase your profits in forex trading.

For instance, a 20 times leverage will yield a return of 30% on a 3% yield. If you have $500 in your account and you have access to 20 times leverage, you can control $10,500. If you try the carry trade strategy from our example, you can earn 3% per annum. By the year-end, your $10,000 investment will be $10300. Take note that you have only invested $1,000 from your pocket, so your actual return is 30%.

But bear in mind that this strategy is only applicable if the value of the currency pair appreciates or not changing. Hence, many forex traders who are using the carry trade strategy focus not only on earning from the interest of the difference between the interest rates, but also for appreciating capital.

For the sake of giving simple examples, we have simplified the transactions given here. It is crucial to take note that there is a minimal difference in interest rate that could lead to huge gains when you apply the leverage. Many forex brokers need a small margin for earning interest rates for implementing the carry trade strategy.

Transactions through carry trade strategy could be complicated through the changes to the exchange rate between the currencies. If the currency is low yielding and it appreciates against a currency that yields higher, the profit you can earn between the two yield might be discarded.

The main reason that this could happen is that for investors, it could be too much to carry the risks of currency that are yielding high. Hence, they usually choose to invest in safer but lower yielding currencies.

Take note that the carry trade strategy is ideal for investors who are looking for long-term profits in the forex trade. Hence, this strategy will make you vulnerable to different changes over time like increasing rates in the currencies with lower yield. This also entices more investors and could result in currency appreciation that could diminish the profits you can make through carry trading.

News Trading

Significant news events around the world could have a large impact on the foreign exchange market, which usually render all analysis meaningless. Take note that the forex market is a 24-hour market, and there is no way to schedule the announcement of news. Changes in the market according to the economy and data could hit any type of trader wherever you are and whichever currency you choose to trade.

If you are in Europe and you want to trade Swiss Francs, you can always read news from Europe. If you prefer Yen or Yuan, then you have to watch for news from Japan, China, and Asia in General. Same goes for other currencies. You have to check the news every day to be updated on any information that could affect your trading.

In the equities market, significant news are often about the publication of corporate earnings, profits, macroeconomic data, profits per share, etc. In the forex market, significant news that affects the market can be announcements from the Central Banks, political events, economic news, inflation reports, and more.

Among the first lessons for beginners in the forex market is when trading, you must be careful in the market during significant news announcements. Nonetheless, you may still find yourself trading during the news, and usually it is not because of being selfish or greedy. Some traders just like the feeling of excitement or adrenaline rush. Some are addicted to the thrill, but most forex traders are only after the profits. After all, you are mainly trading for profits, and the risk is a natural part of the process.

There are always two currencies involved in forex trading. If you are planning to open a position, the news from the two countries must be taken into consideration alongside other foreign news that may affect the currency pair.

For instance, if your decide to trade CHF/NZD, aside from assessing the possible results of the news from Switzerland and New Zealand, and the effect that it could have on the pair, you should also consider significant news from Europe and

Asia or anywhere because the news may cause any movement in the financial markets.

If there was a really good economic data from Australasia, the pair will rally because it means that demand for European products may likely to follow an upward trend. The opposite may happen if the economic conditions in Europe are not that strong. It could affect the worldwide financial market and the traders may likely choose currency alternatives such as USD and Yen.

After establishing the significance of understanding the news and the impact it may have on the price, the next step is to learn how you can use news releases to your advantage. There are two primary methods of using the news trading strategy - the short term and the long term.

Short term news trading is a bit more challenging because of the volatility as well as the tighter stops. More often than not, minutes before and after, there are whipsaws with the rate frantically moving in both directions. Short term news trading is also divided into several strategies.

One method is to sell the currency spike after a bad news. There are instances that even after bad announcements, the price slightly increases for several seconds or even minutes. This is the best time to sell, particularly if it is at some significant resistance or level.

On the other hand, buying after bad news, because of past good data may cause a currency pair to form an uptrend. Even though infrequent, worse than expected news should not be ignored, although this will not affect the general outlook of the situation. Hence, after an initial fall, you should look to buy the immediate response from the market.

In looking for long-term trading opportunities according on economic news, it is crucial to assess both the previous and current data. This is because there are instances that news may take weeks or months to be significantly absorbed by the market. You can use the information to see a larger picture and the impact that it may have on the currency you want to trade. The long term trends are built by fundamental factors that are founded on numerous economic pieces over a specific period of time.

For example, the currency pair GBP/USD has started an uptrend a year ago, and this trend continued ever since. On the other hand, EUR/GBP is following a falling trend for some time now. Take note that these trends have not started out right after.

This has been made possible by the economic data, which came out from Britain during the previous two years or even longer. Majority of the news was about the expected recovery of the economy of Britain long before the trend began to form. Through careful analysis and projection, a trader should have placed his bet on the British Pound and gained from around 2000 pips.

Market Momentum

All forex traders have their own style in trading - some may be bearish, and some may be bullish. Hence, market sentiment is the style of the different traders combined, which produces the general condition of the market.

There are instances that every indicator is pointing in a specific direction but the market is moving in the opposite. There are instances that the fundamental condition of the economy can be considered as bearish for a particular currency, and nevertheless, it keeps on fluctuating upwards in comparison with other currencies.

One example of this is the high movement of the USD/EUR that started in 2012 until early 2017. The European economy in general was not progressing with many member countries still suffering the effects of the recession, inflation falling, and political unrest in some countries. In the US, the economy was recovering in spite of the fair conditions in Europe, the currency pair still rises to an average of 1.40.

It is crucial for forex beginners to be familiar with market sentiment. You will not only be able to read the market sentiment in general, but you can also successfully trade and make profits not only in the foreign exchange market but also in other commodities as well. More often than not, the market sentiment is easy to analyze, because you only need to focus on the primary trend of a particular pair such as the good trend in EUR/USD between 2012 and 2014.

You will surely encounter some tips on forex trading on the importance of the trend as an indicator in forex trading. Somehow, this is true as the trend will allow you to find out the market sentiment. But there are times that trends can be difficult to read. For instance, a day trader who trades every 15 minutes to one hour, may see the trend pointing in single trend. But hours later, the trend may change and so you can lose money.

Trends can really change fast. The larger trends within the daily or four-hour chart could have been trending in the opposing direction, and so the trend that a day trader might be looking at could just be the larger trend's correction.

Hence, before you place an order according to a lower chart timeframe, you have to check the larger charts first. Through this, you will be able to sense the market sentiment and find the pairs you can position your bets on.

Why Focus on One Currency Pair?

Focusing on a single currency pair one at a time is a good way to become familiar with the general market sentiment. Through this, you can gradually master reading currency pairs. Many lucrative forex traders are successfully trading according on their price action sense. In this strategy, you must keep track of how quick a specific pair is moving in two directions.

When the uptrend is quicker than the downtrend, it means that the market is more open to buy immediately, which indicates a more bullish general market sentiment. In addition, you can also monitor how a currency pair responds to financial news that is relevant for the currency pair.

For instance, if the economy in the UK is good, the GBP/USD could bounce up according to the recovering economic data. This signifies a more bearish general market sentiment.

The market sentiment can even be more bearish when the recent announcement in the economy has not yet progressed to form an uptrend.

If you are trading in stocks, you could assess traded volume since the stock market is focused on the stock floor. Take note that this is not true when it comes to forex market investing.

In the foreign exchange spot market, the ideal volume indicator is the COT or Commitments of Traders Report, which is released every 7:30 GMT Fridays. This report contains the net long and short trades of non-commercial and commercial trades in the futures forex market. By reading the COT, you could assess how the market players are positioning, which will have an impact on the forex market.

In general, going with the trend is the best form of trading in the forex market. Through this logic, it is clear that you sell when there are more net shorts, and you buy once there are more net longs. However, there are instances that it is ideal to just ignore the trend. If the buying signals are considered in the extremes, you might need to wait for a while or sell if needed.

If every trader has purchased in the market, there are very few traders who could buy, and so a currency will not be able to follow an uptrend if there is not enough buying activities. Hence, a reversal is imminent because the currencies could close the buying positions. It is also ideal to bet on this report or indicator for long term or medium trend trading, since it comes out every week. When you're into short-term trading, this report can help you in evaluating the trends.

Global Events

Monitoring worldwide events are crucial in sensing the mood of the market. Many of these events may happen on one continent and may seem irrelevant to a currency pair that you are trading. Nonetheless, the whole world is now connected thanks to the power of the Internet, and so any news that is considered globally significant has the possibility to have any impact on the market, especially in the foreign exchange market.

For instance, the rise of ISIS in the Middle East has a significant effect on leading currencies around the globe. When you think about it, CHF has in no way related to the crisis in the Middle East. But as a safe and stable currency, it has surged higher because of the fear of another world war.

In summary, market sentiment is a crucial indicator that you can use in trading in the foreign exchange market as well as other financial markets. All these indicators could establish the sentiment for traders to decide on their strategy.

This can be really challenging for a beginner, but if you want to be profitable in the forex market, it is crucial to have an in-depth learning and try these proven fundamental strategies.

At this point, you should have a basic idea on the general economic and fundamental concepts that form the basis of the foreign exchange market and affect the movement of the currencies.

A key concept that you should learn from this Chapter is that the countries and their currencies, like companies, are continuously changing their values according to fundamental indicators such as interest rates and economic progress. As a beginner in the forex market, you should also have an idea how specific economic factors could affect the currency of a country.

In the next chapter, we will discuss technical analysis as well as the related strategies on how to pick trades in the forex market by looking into the technical indicators.

Chapter 8 - Technical Analysis and Technical Strategies in Forex Trading

"What seems too high and risky to the majority generally goes higher and what seems low and cheap generally goes lower." - William O'Neil

Among the fundamental concepts of technical analysis is that the future price movement could be predicted by looking into past movements.

Because the foreign exchange market is a 24-hour market, you get a chance to assess a huge volume of data, which you can use to measure the price activity, which increases the statistical significance of the projection.

Many investors and traders in the forex market are using technical tools like indicators, charts, and trends.

In general, it is crucial to take note that technical analysis interpretation could stay the same regardless of the assets that you are keeping track. In this Chapter, we will discuss the most popular forex strategies based on technical analysis.

Currency Pair Movements

In doing technical analysis in the forex market, you need to determine if a currency pair may follow a trend in a specific spot, or if it has the probability to remain in the range or go against the trend.

A common way to figure out these traits is to place trend lines, which links previous market levels that have derailed the rate from rising up or declining.

These resistance and support levels are popular among "technicals" to find out if the current trend shall continue.

In general, most currency pairs like GBP/USD, USD/CHF, USD/JPY, and EUR/USD have demonstrated the best performances in the past.

On the other hand, the pairs that have shown better likability to follow the ranges are the pairs that don't involve the USD or known as the crosses.

Minimal Rate Inconsistency

There are different players in the foreign exchange market such as large banks and hedge funds. These large players are equipped with complex computer systems to continuously keep track of any inconsistencies between the various currency pairs.

With these programs, it can be rare to see any significant inconsistency to last longer than a matter of seconds. Many traders are using technical analysis because it presumes that all factors that could affect the currency rates such as psychological, social, political, and economic - have already been considered into the present exchange rate by the market.

With many players and with high volume of transactions every day, the trend as well as the capital flow becomes important instead of trying to determine a rate that is mispriced.

Technical Forex Indicators

Forex traders who prefer technical analysis use various indicators alongside resistance and support levels to help them in projecting the movement of the forex rates in the immediate future. Take note that understanding the different technical factors or indicators is crucial and may require further study on your part.

Among the indicators that you should learn well include stochastics, moving averages, Fibonacci retracement, and Bollinger Bands. Take note that these tools are not often used as an independent indicator but rather alongside chart patterns and other indicators.

Fibonacci Indicator

The Fibonacci Indicator is a common indicator used in technical analysis in the forex market. This strategy heavily depend on the pullback and to completely understand how this works, you should revisit your understanding of the forex trend.

In looking at every price action separately, it is quite difficult to look for a pattern. Taking a closer look at the larger picture will allow you to identify the trends.

For hundreds of years, the Fibonacci ratios and numbers have been popular among artists and mathematicians. These figures signify many things in mathematics, in nature, and even in the financial markets.

Although Fibonacci is a classic concept in mathematics, you don't need to be well adept in the subject so you can use these figures in calculating projections in the forex trading platforms. All you have to do is to make a decision according to the lines that appear on the charts.

By taking a closer look on how far the pullback has reached on the Fibonacci scale, we could figure out if the price could pull back again or turn into a bearish or bullish trend. As long as the price will remain above the specific line, you could expect the trends to pull back through a rising trend. When the price crosses the line, you should treat it as a beginning of a bearish trend that will indicate that it is time to close the position.

Horizontal Level Indicator

Horizontal Levels are among the most simple but quite useful concepts trading in the forex market. These are fundamentals in most forex trading strategies and could help you in studying charts. But you can also use them as a separate strategy instead of a mere tool to ride along with other strategies.

In monitoring the most clear-cut price actions and identifying the horizontal levels, you can make profitable trades. In completely becoming familiar with the horizontal levels of advanced charts, you can identify trends that you might have otherwise ignored.

Many forex traders regard horizontal levels as equally essential as price action that is ultimately regarded as the core of forex trading. Evaluating the integration of the change in price as well as the horizontal levels could allow you to be familiar with the trend and project the movement of the market. Even though horizontal levels could be a simple strategy in trading in the forex market, many popular forex traders like

George Soros and Warren Buffet have recognized horizontal levels as a pillar for their strategies.

Horizontal levels could help you spot certain parts on a chart where the change on the trend could likely to happen. This could help you to decide where you could put a stop, or if you want to enter a trade, but you are not sure of the best time in doing so.

Take note that timing is critical in most trading strategies in the forex market and you should take extra caution in evaluating horizontal levels to find the proper time and position a good trade. Take note that horizontal levels are used as a basis for many other forex trading strategies, but when used separately, it is often not sufficient and should be used alongside other forex strategies.

The ideal method in using horizontal levels to your advantage is through the analysis of swing points, which refer to the points where there is a change in trends. By marking the horizontal levels on these places, you can find the prices where there could be a likely change in the trend.

Take note that swing points are more likely to recur themselves. Resistance levels could turn into support levels, and the other way around. When you mark the horizontal levels on your graph, you can project the next point of the swing will likely to happen and exit or enter a trade at the right time.

Ranging Market Indicator

Horizontal levels can be used in ranging markets, which refers to the condition in which the price has clear lower and upper boundaries.

By monitoring the price when it is approaching a limit, you can project with precision the points where the price could be more likely to continue the trend.

It can be hard to predict the price, and may even break down the boundary as you are deciding to enter the trade. But in general, this forex technical strategy is safe and very reliable.

In a chart, the horizontal levels will continue to rise and fall between distinct boundaries. You can mark the boundaries as horizontal levels so you could utilize them for your advantage.

Then, the next move is to wait for the moment that the price will go near the boundaries so you can finally place your trade. Remember, the price will unlikely jump over the horizontal level of the boundary, so you could place a trade hoping for a switch in the trend, and so the price could return to the horizontal level.

If the price is approaching an upper boundary, the trend is usually bearish and so the price will likely go down. On the other hand, when the rate is approaching a lower boundary, the trend is often bullish and an uptrend in the price may happen.

The reward and risk levels could also quite easy to select in this market type. The level of risk must be below or above the boundary that you have entered in the trade from, and the reward level must be on the opposing boundary of the ranging market.

Divergence Indicators

Aside from the market fundamentals, traders and market analysts are using several indicators to determine the price movements of a specific instrument.

Understanding these divergence indicators will provide you a basic approach of detecting patterns and projecting the price trends. Using these indicators is what makes signals in the forex market helpful, as you can use them for live analysis of price action.

Divergence is one such indicator, which can help you to significantly increase your profits in the forex market. The probability of entering in the correct direction at the best time could increase if you use this indicator alongside others such as support or resistance levels, stochastics, RSI, and moving averages.

Just by recognizing the name of the indicator, you could simply know that the divergent approach is a form of trading in deviation or disharmony. The indicators and prices normally follow in a similar direction and also at similar rates.

When the price reaches a high-high trend, the indicator must also reach a high-high trend, and if the price also reaches a low-high trend, then the indicator should follow as well. The same goes for higher lows and lower lows.

When the indicators and the price are not in harmony, then it can be true that some type of change will happen. Therefore, divergence is computed between the lows and highs of the prices. The ideal metrics for trading divergence are volumes, MACD, stochastics, and RSI.

Divergence could be easy to spot, as you only need to draw several lines in a chart. However, there are instances that traders are looking too hard at the charts, which makes them see things that are not actually helpful in making the trade.

For instance, when liquidity is low or during consolidation, some minor divergences between indicators and price could form. However, this doesn't mean you should consider them actual divergences.

Chapter 9 - Basic Forex Trading Skills You Need to Learn

"I think investment psychology is by far the more important element, followed by risk control, with the least important consideration being the question of where you buy and sell." – Tom Basso

There are many ways to become a successful forex trader. For example, if you want to be a forex trader under a financial firm, they usually hire people who have a strong background in the hard sciences, engineering, or math.

In starting your career as a forex trader, there are basic skills you need to learn. This includes the following:

1. Analytical skills
2. Research skills
3. Focus and Control
4. Money management
5. Psychology

Basic Trading Skills

Analytical thinking is a basic skill that every forex trader should have. You must be able to analyze the available data within a limited time frame.

Forex trading is a numbers game and the platform is filled with patterns, indicators, and charts that you need to analyze quickly. You also need to develop your analytical skills so you can easily identify trends in the forex market.

Reading Currency Quote

When you are quoting a currency, you are doing it in relation to the currency of another country in a way that the value is defined by the other currency's value.

Hence, if you want to know the forex rate between the Swiss Francs (CHF) and Chinese Yuan (CNY), the forex quotation will look like this:

CHF/CNY = 6.95

This is known as the currency pair. In this pair, CHF is the base currency, while CNY is the counter currency. The former always has a value of one unit, and the latter is what that one base unit is equivalent in its denomination. This fx pair means that CHF1 = 6.95 Chinese Yuan. So if you have one Swiss Franc, you can buy 6.95 Chinese Yuan. Take note that the fx quote includes the currency symbol for the currency pairs.

You can quote a currency pair either indirectly or directly. An indirect quote is basically when the local currency is the base currency, while a direct quote is basically a forex pair wherein the domestic currency is the quote currency.

Therefore, if you are looking for the United States Dollar as the domestic currency and the Japanese Yen as the foreign currency, an indirect code will be JPY/USD, while a direct quote will be USD/JPY

In a direct quotation, the quoted currency could vary, while the base currency has a default value of one unit. Meanwhile, in the indirect quote, the domestic currency has a default value of one unit, while the foreign currency has a variable value.

For instance, if Japanese Yen is the domestic unit, a direct quote will be 109.37 USD/JPY, which means that 1 unit of USD can buy JPY 109.37. The indirect for this will be inverse (1/109.37), 0.0091 JPY/USD, which means with 1 JPY, you can buy USD 0.0091.

In the fx spot market, most currencies are traded against the USD, and this is often referred to as currency base. These are all direct quotes and true to the above CHF/CNY that indicates 1 CHF is equal to 6.95 CNY.

You must remember that not all currencies have the USD as the base. The currencies used by the British Commonwealth such as the New Zealand Dollar, Australian Dollar, and the British pound are all identified as the base currency against the USD. This is how we also quote the Euro. For these situations, the USD is positioned as the counter currency, and the fx rate is known as an indirect quote. Hence, EUR to USD is quoted as 1.19, because one unit of Euro can buy 1.19 USD.

The exchange currency rates are quoted up to four digits after the decimal place. One exception to this is the Japanese Yen, because this currency is quoted only up to two decimal places.

If a currency quote is given without the USD as a component, this is known as cross currency. The most popular cross currency pairs are the EUR/CHF, EUR/JPY, and the EUR/GBP. In general, currency pairs expand the trading horizons in the fx market. But you should bear in mind that they are not that much popular compared to the currency pair that uses USD as the base currency.

Buying and Selling Price

Like in stock markets, if you are trading currency pairs, you have to refer to the buying rate (bid) and the selling price (ask). Take note that these are still in relation to the base currency. If your strategy is to long (buying a currency pair) the asking price refers to the rate of quoted currency, which should be paid so you can purchase one unit of the base currency, or how much the market is willing to sell a unit of the base currency in reference to the currency quote.

On the other hand, when you go short (selling) a currency pair the bid rate signifies how much of the quoted currency you can get when you sell a unit of the base currency or how much the market is willing to shell out for the currency (quoted) in reference to the currency base.

Remember, the figure on the left of the slash is the bid rate, while the next two digits to the right of the slash are the asking price. Take note that it is customary to quote only the last two digits of the full price. The bid is also smaller compared to the asking price. Below is an example:

USD/CHF = 1.3000/05

Ask = 1.3005

Bid = 1.3000

Buying this fx pair signifies that you like to purchase the base currency, and so you have to refer to the asking price to know how much in Swiss Francs the market will charge for US dollars. Based on our asking price, you can purchase $ 1.00 with 1.3005 Swiss Francs, which is the currency that you are quoting.

But if you want to sell this fx pair or in other words you want to sell the currency base using the quoted currency, you have to refer to the bid. This signifies that the market will purchase $1 base currency for a price that is equivalent of 1.3000 Swiss Francs, which is the currency that you are quoting.

The base currency (whichever you are quoting first) always refer to the one in which we are conducting the transaction. This means, you can either buy or sell the currency base. You can refer to the specific currency pair rate in order to find the price depending on what currency you like to use for selling or buying the base with.

Research Skills

In trading in the forex market, you should not trade on an impulse. You must be confident with your strategy and you can do this through research. In the past, you can do a background check on the hottest currency pairs by reading books, newspapers, and other traditional forms of information sources.

But with the advent of the World Wide Web, there are now countless sources of information that you can use for your research. However, not all of these sources are reliable and can guide you to become successful forex traders. In choosing a source to consult, make certain that this covers the currency pairs to buy or if it is time to sell your currencies based on different factors such as technical and fundamental analysis.

There are also reliable newspapers and publications that you can read, which includes interpretation of global news and how the current events could affect the forex market. Forex trading involves revisiting past basic economics, because politics can also affect the behavior of forex players. Hence, it is crucial that you are updated with significant non-financial news from around the world.

In order to develop a solid foundation in forex trading, you must be updated with important technical and fundamental developments in the industry. Successful forex traders usually have a thirst for information as well as the drive to look for all relevant data, which could affect the trade.

Many traders even maintain a monitoring platform to keep up with major news breakthrough that can have considerable impact not only in the forex market but also in the global financial scene.

Focus and Control

Focus is another important skill for forex traders, which can increase the more that you practice it. With the emergence of numerous online resources promising to guide you on forex trading, you should be able to develop how to identify and focus your lens on the actionable trends that could affect your trade.

There are forex traders that are only focusing on specific types of currency pairs so they can put all of their efforts in projecting the movement of the trade. By focusing on these currencies, traders can develop competitive advantage compared to traders who don't focus on their trades.

Meanwhile, a successful trader should also learn how to control their emotions and follow specific strategy or trading plan. This is crucial in handling risks in forex trades by taking profits at specific points or using stop losses. There are strategies in place that allow traders to lose a bit on bad trades but gain more revenue from ideal trades. Bad traders are usually affected by their emotions, which influence the strategic implementation of their trading plan.

Risk Management

Risk Management is a skill that you should master to safeguard your trading capital from losses. This must be integrated in your trading strategy as early as you can in your forex trading career. Risk management covers strategies such as risk to reward, scaling trades, and stop losses. Mastering this skill will allow you to obtain higher profits and prevent losing money.

For instance, many successful traders don't risk more than 2 per cent of their funds in a single trade. This will safeguard your account from any significant downturn and will allow you to safely trade using leverage.

Psychology

Successful traders are not only adept in the mathematics behind the forex trading platform. They are also masters of understanding the psychology of people behind the trade. Aside from observing the possible behavior of market players, a forex trader should also overcome psychological aspects such as greed and fear.

In forex trading, you should learn how to follow the rules of the game without allowing your emotions to distract your game plan. It is not easy to become a successful forex trader, but if you work through your plan and master yourself, you can win the game through skills and discipline.

Chapter 10 - How to Set-up Your Forex Trading Account and Begin Trading

"It's not what we do once in a while that shapes our lives. It's what we do consistently."

–Anthony Robbins

At this point, you may feel that you can now begin to trade in the foreign exchange market.

Make sure that you understand this Chapter so you can learn the important steps to set-up forex account and then begin trading currencies.

We have also included other important considerations that you must understand before you open up your forex trading account.

Gearing Up With a Forex Practice Account

For beginners in the forex market, the best way to gear up in this new opportunity is to use a practice account.

Many online forex brokers provide free trials so you can sign up with a trading account and immediately experience real-time price action without spending your own real money first.

In most practice accounts, you will be provided with a virtual cash that you can make trades. The risk will be zero and you can take advantage of the experience as you learn how forex trading works.

With a practice account, you will actually see how prices fluctuate at different times of the day and you can see how currency pairs may vary from each other.

While trading in a practice account, you should alongside monitor the news relevant to the currencies you are trading. This will provide you an insight on how the forex market will react to news releases.

Aside from evaluating the market movement, you may also start trading in real-time conditions in the market without the risk of losing your money and you can also try various trading strategies to see if they work in your condition.

You can also improve your own understanding on how margin trading and leverage works and you can experience managing opening positions and you'll get a chance using various orders.

Most forex brokers will allow 30-day trials when you can also access charts and other technical supplements.

Before you sign up for a full membership, try to open practice accounts first with different forex brokers. Explore different features and capacities of these platforms. Also take note that different forex brokers have different trading policies.

Setting Up a Forex Trading Account

Forex trading is quite similar to stock market trading because you have first to open your own trading account. Similar to the stock market, every forex account as well as the services you can take advantage of can be different. Hence, it is crucial that you look for the most suitable platform for you. In this Chapter, we will discuss the important factors that you consider when you are choosing a foreign exchange account.

Trading Leverage

When we speak of leverage, we refer to the opportunity to take control of bigger amounts of cash with minimal capital from your own pocket. The leverage level is directly proportional to the risk level. Take note that the leverage amount on a platform could be different according to the features of the account on its own. However, the most popular one is the 50:1 leverage. Some accounts could offer a maximum leverage of 250:1.

For example, a maximum leverage of 100:1 signifies that in each dollar that you hold in the brokerage account, you can use up to $100. For instance, if you have an account balance of $100, the brokerage can allow you to trade as much as $10,000 in the fx. This leverage could also define the total amount that you can hold in your account or your margin for trading a specific amount. In the stock market, the margin is

152

often at 50 per cent and the leverage could be 50:1, which can be at least 2 per cent.

In general, leverage is regarded as a primary advantage of trading in the foreign exchange market, because this will allow you to create substantial gains with minimal capital. But leverage could also have extreme downsides when a trade is moving in the opposite direction, because the losses could also be big.

With this leverage type, there is always the actual probability that your losses are higher than what you have invested, even though most accounts have safeguard stops to prevent the account from hitting negative. As such, it is crucial that you take note of this when you open a brokerage account, and once you identify your preferred leverage, you could understand the involved risks.

Fees and Commissions

Another major advantage of forex platforms is that investing through them could be done through a commission, which is unlike stock market accounts where you need to pay a broker a certain fee for every trade. You are now directly dealing with market players and you don't have to pass through another layer such as brokers.

Every time that you enter a trade, it is the market makers, which can seize the spread. Hence, when the ask/bid for a forex market is 1.5300/50, the market maker can capture between the difference between the points.

In setting up your own forex account, be sure to take note that every firm has various spreads on currency pairs that you trade. Even though they are usually different by only several pips, this could be substantial when you are planning to do a lot of trading. Hence, in setting up an account, be certain that you are aware of the pip and spread of specific currency pairs that you are interested in trading.

Other Factors

You must take note that there are several differences between every forex platform and the programs or software that they are offering. Hence, it is crucial to review every firm before you make a commitment. Every forex trading company may offer various levels of programs and services including the fees beyond and above the actual costs of trading. Moreover, because of the less strict conditions in the foreign exchange market, you should find a reliable firm. When you are also not completely confident to trade with real cash, you can also try trading in practice accounts or demos.

How to Start Trading in the Forex Market

After understanding the most crucial factors in opening your own forex account, it is time to look into what specifically you could trade within the platform. The two primary methods in trading in the forex market includes the actual trading (selling and buying) of forex pairs, in which you short a currency and long another.

Another method is via buying the derivatives that monitor the fluctuations of particular currency pair. These strategies are quite similar to the common techniques used in the stock market. Basically, buying and selling the currency pair is the most popular method, much in a similar manner that many traders are buying and selling currency units.

In this setting, a trader may hope that the currency pair's value will change in a profitable way. If you choose to short a pair, it signifies that you are betting on the possibility that the pair's value will fall. For instance, let's assume that you want a short position for the USD/JPY pair.

You can make profits when the value of the fx pair goes down, and you will lose your investment if it rises. This pair will rise if USD increases its price against the JPY, therefore it is actually a trust on the JPY.

Another alternative is to use futures and options, which are derivative products, so you can make money from the currency value changes. If you purchase a currency pair option, you can gain the privilege to buy a pair on a specific rate prior to a setting of point.

Meanwhile, a futures forex contract could build the agreement to purchase the currency pair at a specific point. These trading strategies are often employed by more experienced traders, but as a beginner, you should be aware of them.

Order Types

In looking for a new trading position, you may have to use a market order or a limit order, which are actually similar when you are placing a new position in the stock market. A market order can provide you the capacity to acquire the currency at specific exchange rate that it is presently trading in the foreign exchange market. On the other hand, the limit order will allow you to identify a specific entry price.

If you are already holding an open position in the market, you may have to consider employing a take profit order, so you could lock in your gains. For instance, let us assume that you are already sure that the USD/GBP will react at 1.8700, but you are not completely certain that the price will rise any higher. You can use a take-profit order that will immediately close your position if the price hits 1.8700, which will lock in your profits.

156

The stop loss order is also a tool that you can use when you want to hold the open positions. This will allow you to figure out if the price could decline prior to the closing of the position and more losses could be accumulated. Hence, if the USD/GBP rate starts to drop, the investor may put a stop-loss, which could halt the position to avoid any further loss.

When you are also trading in the stock market, you will realize that the order types that you could enter in the forex trading accounts are quite similar. It is crucial to be familiar with these orders before you actually place your very first trade in the foreign exchange market.

Conclusion

Congratulations for finishing this book until the end.

At this point, you should already have enough understanding of forex trading and figure out if this is a suitable revenue channel for you.

Hopefully, the lessons that you have learned in this book will help you become a successful forex day trader and have a prosperous career.

As a summary, I would like you to remember the following pointers that we have discussed in this book:

- The forex market is the product of important historical events that result in designating USD as the primary reserve currency to replace gold. This is the reason why major currencies are always pitted against the dollar.

- At its core, forex trading is all about speculating the value of one currency against another. Similar to trading stocks or other financial instruments, forex trading is speculative with the hope that it will increase its value and you as a trader will make a profit.

- In the forex market, it is always important to be mindful of liquidity, which refers to the market interest level or the level of trading volume available at any point in time for a specific asset or security. The deeper or the higher the liquidity, the easier and faster it is to trade a security.

- Forex trading involves trading currency pairs with names that involve two different currencies. Currency pairs have nicknames or abbreviations that refer to the pair but does not necessarily involve the individual currencies.

- At any given moment, any number of real-world forces are at work in the forex market. This includes geopolitical events, interest rate decisions, and economic data.

- The primary economic theories found in the forex market are more about the parity settings. Basically, parity refers to the economic justification of the price at which the currency pairs must be traded according to important factors such as interest rates and inflation.

- In the stock market, fundamental analysis measures the true value of a company. A fundamentalist (one who mainly use fundamental analysis) base his decision to invest or trade in stocks according to the calculation.

- Many investors and traders in the forex market are using technical tools like indicators, charts, and trends.

- In starting your career as a forex trader, there are basic skills you need to learn. This includes analytical skills, research skills, focus and control, financial management, and psychology.

- Forex trading is quite similar to stock market trading because you have first to open your own trading account. Similar to the stock market, every forex account as well as the services you can take advantage of can be different. So, it is important that you look for the most suitable platform for you.

While this beginner's guide is only a small glimpse of all you need to know about forex trading, I hope that you have gained enough insight into this subject.

I also encourage you to learn more about the intricacies of the forex world and currency pairs that you want to trade. You must continue the best strategies that are suitable for you.

Thanks again, and good luck!

Thank you

Before you go, I just wanted to say thank you for purchasing my book.

You could have picked from dozens of other books on the same topic but you took a chance and chose this one.

So, a HUGE thanks to you for getting this book and for reading all the way to the end.

Now I wanted to ask you for a small favor. **Could you please consider posting a review on the platform? Reviews are one of the easiest ways to support the work of authors.**

This feedback will help me continue to write the type of books that will help you get the results you want. So if you enjoyed it, please let me know.

www.ingramcontent.com/pod-product-compliance
Lightning Source LLC
Chambersburg PA
CBHW071416210326
41597CB00020B/3523